I0125708

David Downie

The Lone Star

The History of the Telugu Mission of the American Baptist Missionary Union

David Downie

The Lone Star
The History of the Telugu Mission of the American Baptist Missionary Union

ISBN/EAN: 9783337033620

Printed in Europe, USA, Canada, Australia, Japan

Cover: Foto ©ninafisch / pixelio.de

More available books at **www.hansebooks.com**

THE LONE STAR.

THE

HISTORY OF THE TELUGU MISSION

OF THE

AMERICAN BAPTIST MISSIONARY UNION

BY

DAVID DOWNIE, D. D.,
MISSIONARY AT NELLORE.

PHILADELPHIA :
AMERICAN BAPTIST PUBLICATION SOCIETY,
1420 Chestnut Street.

Entered, according to Act of Congress, in the year 1893, by the
AMERICAN BAPTIST PUBLICATION SOCIETY,
In the Office of the Librarian of Congress, at Washington.

CONTENTS.

PREFACE.

"THE history of the Telugu Mission," says Dr. Bright, of the "Examiner," "is interesting even to romance. That history should be told in every church and Sunday-school as an inspiration to greater hope and patience in all our work. . . . Would not the prayerful consideration of so memorable and blessed a history of missionary triumphs, as is furnished by the Telugu Mission, be the highest possible incentive to renewed consecration and a further development of the grace of giving?" It is with some such hope as this that the writer has undertaken the task of furnishing a fuller history of the Mission than has yet been written, and thus afford its friends additional facilities for "the prayerful consideration" of God's wonder-working power among the Telugus.

It was only after repeated efforts had be n made to induce another, in all respects better qualified, to undertake this work, that the writer consented to do it. The only advantage he possesses over the one first selected is a long residence among the people and an active participation in the work he seeks to describe.

In presenting this book to the friends of missions, the writer claims very little in the way of original authorship. Like most books of its kind, it partakes largely of the nature

5

of a compilation.   He has not hesitated to take from any and
every source within his reach facts bearing on the Mission's
history.   Many of these facts were gathered from conversations with native Christians who were school children in Mr.
Day's time.   Some have been told before, though not always
correctly ; some are here given for the first time.

The author is under especial obligation to Miss M. M. Day,
of Madras, for the reading of her father's private letters ;
also to Dr. Clough for the use of his Missionary Magazines
from 1864 to 1873 ; likewise to the Missionary Union's Jubilee
Volume and Magazine, Dr. McKenzie's "Lone Star," and to
several of the missionaries who have aided him in various
ways ; for all of which aid he extends his warmest thanks.

NELLORE, INDIA, 1892.

LANGUAGE MAP OF INDIA.

Scale of English Statute Miles

REFERENCE KEY.

1 SANTÁL (WITH MALER, DRAVIDIAN)
2 MUNDARI
3 HO AND KÓL
4 BHUMIJ
5 KHARRIA
6 JUANG
7 KORWA
8 KUR AND KÚRKU
9 SAWARA
10 KOTA AND TODA (Dravidian)

Note

The *Aryan* languages are distinguished by red tints .... red tints
The *Dravidian* .... green ....
The *Kolarian* .... brown ...
The *Burmo-Tibetan* .... blue ....
The *Khasi* .... yellow ..

THE HISTORY OF THE TELUGU MISSION.

CHAPTER I.

THE COUNTRY AND PEOPLE.

The Aryan invasion of India. Previous invasions. Derivation of name—
Telugu. The three "lingas." The country and its location. The Monsoons. The climate. The occupants of the country. English rule in India.
Blessings derived therefrom. The agriculture of the country. The origin
of the Telugus. The castes of the people. Their physical characteristics.
Their language. Not Sanskrit. The population of the country. Number
uncertain. Not migratory. Telugus in Burma. Burmese civilization
from them. The religion of the Telugus. The Vedas and Brahmans The
laws of Manu. The numerous gods. Idol worship. Not originally a part
of worship. Now universal. Caste adherence. Numerous trade castes.
Not wholly observed by all. Pariahs even rising. Leveling by railroads.
Influence of mission schools. Caste still a factor.

WHEN the great Aryan race first invaded India
(B. C. 1500), it settled in the neighborhood of
the river Sindhu. The Persians called it Hindhu and the
Greeks called the people Ἰνδοί. Thus we get the words
Hindu and Hindustan which were originally applied only
to the regions of the Indus. As the Aryans spread farther
and farther south and east, the name followed them, until
now Hindustan is applied to the entire peninsula of India.

Previous to the incursions of the Aryans, India had
been invaded by several mixed races from Central Asia,
Tartary, and Tibet. Some of them were Scythian and
some Mongolian. Among them were what are now

called the Dravidian races of South India. The term Dravidas was first applied to the Tamils only, but now includes the Tamils, Telugus, Canarese, Malayalams, Gonds, and some others.

The Telugus were originally called by the Aryan conquerors, Andhras; but the Andhras were divided into two nations, one of which was called the Kalingas, who occupied the seaboard, while the Andhras occupied the interior northwest portion of the Telugu country. Although the Andhras were better known to the Aryans, and were probably the more cultured of the two nations speaking a common tongue, yet it is from the Kalingas that the modern term Telugu comes. From Kalinga came Talinga and Tenugu—the name which is even now frequently used by pundits for Telugu.

The favorite derivation of Telugu pundits for Telugu is Trilinga, or "country of the three lingas." One of the earliest of Buddhistic writers frequently designates the Telugu country Trilinga, and describes Kalinga as a portion of Trilinga. Ptolemy also speaks of a country in India as Τό καὶ Τρίλιγγον βασίλειον, "The kingdom of the three lingas."

These three celebrated lingas are said to be at Kalahastry in the south, Sreesalem in the west, and Dracharamu in the north. But a better known boundary of the Telugu country is Pulicat, about twenty-five miles north of Madras in the south, Chicacole in the north, and Udghiri in the Nizam's dominions in the northwest.

The country thus described contains about seventy-three thousand seven hundred and twenty-eight square miles, and is for the most part flat. It is, however, divided by a range of mountains running generally north and south called the Eastern Ghauts. The highest peak is called Penchalaconda and rises to a height of three thousand six hundred feet, and next to it is Udayagiri Droog, which is three thousand and sixty-nine feet. The difference of temperature between the plains and the summits of these hills is about ten degrees. The portion of the Telugu country embraced in the Nizam's dominions, while also level, is on a higher plain, Secunderabad being two thousand feet above the level of the sea, while Nellore is only sixty feet.

The Telugu country lies between latitude fourteen and eighteen north, and hence twice in the year, about May 10th and August 1st, the sun is vertical. If there were no counteracting influences, the temperature would be pretty nearly equal in all parts of the Telugu country; but the trade winds called monsoons exert such an influence on the climate that it is difficult to give a general statement. Thus while May and June are the hottest months in Nellore, March and April are the hottest west of the Ghauts. In Secunderabad the thermometer falls to fifty-four degrees in December, while in Nellore sixty-four degrees mark the lowest record, and that very early in the morning. The average temperature of the Nellore District is eighty-two degrees, and this is probably not far from the average of the whole Telugu country. The average maximum temperature is about ninety-five degrees, though in some sections it frequently reaches one hundred and ten degrees in the shade.

There are two monsoons during the year, i. e., the prevailing winds blow from one of two directions throughout the year. The southwest monsoon is supposed to begin about the middle of February, but its effects are not very perceptible until early in June. It lasts till about the middle of August, when the northeast monsoon is supposed to set in, though here again the effects are not felt until the middle of October. These monsoons usually set in with high winds followed by heavy rains. The rains are not a *necessary* sequence of the monsoon, but they are so general that when they do not come—as is sometimes the case—the monsoon is said to have failed. The rains of an average monsoon last about six weeks, during which time nearly the entire year's supply of rain falls. But some sections of the Telugu country share in both monsoons. The average rain-fall of the Nellore District is about thirty-five inches. In Madras it is forty-one inches. Thus it will be seen how vitally important are these monsoon rains to a country so dependent as India is upon its agriculture. Another effect of the monsoons is their influence on the climate. With the sun so nearly vertical the year round, but for the monsoons the climate would be simply unbearable. By a glance at the map, it will be seen that the southwest monsoon coming over the Indian Ocean reaches India on the west coast. Laden with moisture, these winds strike the Western Ghauts; the moisture is condensed and falls in torrents of rain. The earth thus cooled and the cool ocean breezes give to the west coast a climate very much like that of Burma—not exactly cool, but certainly cooler than that of the east coast. But while these ocean winds cool and refresh the West, they have a very different effect upon the East. Long before they reach the Bay of Bengal a vertical sun has converted them into what are called "land or hot winds."

It is all but impossible to convey to one who has not experienced it the effect of these hot winds. A huge prairie
fire within a mile or two of your dwelling, with a wind
blowing in its direction at the rate of thirty or forty miles
an hour, would furnish some idea of the effect. Toward
evening, however, a counteraction usually takes place. The
intense heat of the sun during the day so rarifies the
atmosphere that the cooler air of the ocean rushes in and
gives, at this season, what is called the east breeze, which
lasts a few hours; but as the earth cools down the prevailing west wind resumes its sway.

About the middle of October, the northeast monsoon
sets in, but the relative effects on the east and west coasts
are not exactly reversed; for by this time the sun has
traveled several degrees south, so that while the west coast
has a "land wind" it cannot have the "hot" winds experienced on the east. The only compensation for this is
that the "hot winds" while very trying are not generally
regarded as unhealthful. Following the rains of the northeast monsoon there is a brief season of ten or twelve weeks
of delightful weather.

Previous to the Aryan invasions, the Telugu country, or
Telingana as it was then called, was governed by its own
kings; but while there is no evidence that they were ever
conquered by the Aryans. the latter seem gradually to
have assumed control of the country. The Aryans were
in turn displaced by the Mohammedan and Mogul conquerors. Since the occupation of the English, in the early half
of the eighteenth century, the greater part of the Telugu
country has been under direct British rule. The northwest portion, however, is under the government of the

Nizam of Hyderabad.   This native prince is to some extent independent, but he is aided in his government by a British resident who guards the interests of the British Government.   A large British force is maintained at Secunderabad, supported at the expense of the Nizam. The force serves the double purpose of protecting British India from the Nizam, and the Nizam from a foreign invasion.

Much has been said against British rule in India by transient visitors, and even by those who have never seen it or carefully studied its history.   "Spoliation of India," " Bleeding to death," etc., are among the favorite epithets employed by such critics.   But nothing could be more unjust or farther from the truth.   For many centuries before the British came, India was the scene of invasion after invasion, war upon war, conquest upon conquest. Scarcely a year passed in which thousands were not slain. The Aryans, with all their boasted civilization, made warfare and bloodshed a part of their religion.   In the Rig-Veda, Indra was invited to "quaff the soma-juice abundantly," and urged to destroy its enemies.   "Hurl thy hottest thunderbolt upon them!   Uproot them!   Cleave them asunder ! "   The Mahabharata, the great epic poem of the Hindus, is simply a history of successive wars ending in the almost total destruction of the contending parties. Nor were the Mohammedan invasions less destructive or cruel.   During seven hundred years, the warring races of Central Asia and Afghanistan kept up perpetual warfare, pillage, and cruel massacre.   In twenty-three years during the last century, no less than six invasions of India took place.   The first was by the Persians who, in a single

forenoon, are said to have hacked to pieces thirty thous-
and men, women, and children in the streets of Delhi.
Then followed five successive invasions of Afghans, no less
horrible. They sacked and destroyed the temples and
murdered the priests ; they burned whole cities with their
inhabitants, slaying with sword and lance those who
attempted to escape.

Whatever else may be said of British rule in India, it
has at least put a stop to these bloody invasions, and has
given the country peace. The annual cost to the inhabitants of India for maintaining the army which secured and
perpetuates this peace is about one rupee (about fifty
cents) per head. But the value of the produce even from
a single province reclaimed from devastating hordes of in-
vaders more than covers the cost of the entire Indian
army.

But peace is only one of the many blessings England has secured to India. Crime has been repressed ;
thugism has been rooted out ; the cruel rites of suttee
(widow burning) have been abolished ; human sacrifices to
Hindu demons have been prohibited ; law and order have
been established ; the health of the people has been pro-
moted ; famines have been mitigated, and the resources of
the country developed ; education has been extended ; the
liberty of the press has been conceded ; and absolute freedom of worship and propagation of religion granted without regard to creed or nationality. Under such a government, it is safe to say, the country never was better
ruled and the people never were more prosperous, con-
tented, or happy.

As in nearly all other parts of India, agriculture is the

chief industry of the Telugu country. In the low lands
along the coast, and especially on the river deltas, rice is
the chief product. For rice cultivation large supplies of
water are a necessity. During long dry seasons, the
fields become baked, so that they must be submerged before
they can be plowed. The seed is sown upon the water,
and during the entire growth, the fields have to be almost
daily flooded. This could not he done by depending upon
the periodic rains. Hence, artifical means have to be employed for storing up the vast quantity of water that falls
during the rainy seasons. For this purpose extensive
irrigation works are to be found all over India. To give
some idea of these works, those in the vicinty of Nellore
may be described. First, there is the great Nellore tank
or lake, partly natural and partly artificial. It is nearly
round, is about six miles in diameter, and when full has
about three feet of water. Part of the water comes from
the rains and part from the river Pennar. On this tank
four thousand acres of land are dependent for their
supply of water. Across the Pennar, close to the town, is
an anicut which serves the double purpose of a bridge
and a dam for diverting the water into irrigating channels.
By this means about three thousand acres of land are furnished with water during most of the year. Twenty miles
farther up the river, a second anicut has lately been constructed. It cost three million seven hundred thousand
rupees, or say one million five hundred thousand dollars.
It has thrown into cultivation forty-five thousand acres of
waste land and forty-five thousand acres heretofore only
partially cultivated for lack of water. The annual tax
for the use of this water is about two dollars to two dollars

and twenty-five cents per acre. It is easy to see what an immense gain to the productiveness of the country these irrigation works are. They cost the country nothing except the tax for the use of water. Government borrows the money and repays it from the revenue derived from the lands which the works benefit. Rice, however, is by no means the only or even the chief product of the whole Telugu country. The proportion of irrigated land in the Madras Presidency is only twenty-three per cent., hence more than seventy-five per cent. is under what is called "dry cultivation," that is, lands which are cultivated with the ordinary rains. On these lands wheat, raghi, jonna, and other food grains, oil-seeds, cotton, and tobacco are among the chief products. In some sections, dry crops are the rule, wet cultivation being the exception.

The Telugus are of Scythian origin. This has sometimes been disputed on philological grounds, but is now pretty generally admitted. When these Scythian colonists entered India is not known. The most that can be said is, that previous to the first Aryan invasions the Scythians were in possession of the land; B. C. 2000 is probably the latest date that can be given. As the Aryans spread over Southern India, being a more powerful and more civilized race, they gradually combined the two races into what is called the Hindu people. The Aryan Brahmans and Kshetryas retained the first and second places or castes; the better portion of the Scythians were admitted into the third or Vysia caste; but the majority were left in the fourth or Sudra caste. Hence the latter claim to be the only true Telugus. Whether the Pariahs or outcaste class came in with the Scythians, or at an earlier period, or whether they may be called the aborigines of the country, it is quite impossible to say. Physically they differ in no respect from other Telugus, except that usually they are darker-skinned.

How far these five classes whom we call Telugus, because living in the Telugu country and speaking the Telugu tongue, have amalgamated, would be a very difficult problem. The laws of the Brahmans forbid the marriage of one caste with another, but unfortunately this by no means decides the question.

Physically the Telugus compare favorably with the other races of South India. The Reddis, or farming class of the Sudras, are a particularly fine-looking set of men. They are tall, erect, and well proportioned. Generally the Telugus are of average height, but the lower limbs are much more slender than those of the average European. Telugu women are rather below the average height, and much more slender than Europeans; but they are equal, and in some respects, superior to their southern sisters, the Tamils. They are modest in their manners, and their dress is particularly graceful and becoming.

The Telugu language ranks at least second in what are known as the Dravidian languages of South India. Tamil being probably more ancient, as it certainly is more copious and more independent of foreign words, has generally been assigned the first place. In euphony and melodious sweetness, however, Telugu deservedly holds the first rank, not only of Dravidian, but of all other languages of India. From this latter quality it has been likened to the Italian, and has in fact been called the "Italian of the East." As might be expected from the dominating influence of the

Aryans, the Telugu, in common with the Tamil and other Dravidian languages, has incorporated a large number of Sanskrit terms. Of the higher, or literary Telugu, fully one-third of the vocabulary is Sanskrit. The proportion is less, however, in the language of the common people. It is chiefly because of this large Sanskrit element in the Dravidian languages that some have claimed for them an Aryan origin. But Dr. Caldwell, admittedly the foremost scholar in the Dravidian languages, in his comparative grammar says on this point : "The supposition of the derivation of the Dravidian languages from Sanskrit though entertained in the past generation by a Colebrook, a Carey, and a Wilkins, is now known to be entirely destitute of foundation. Those Orientalists, though deeply learned in Sanskrit and well acquainted with the idioms of Northern India, were unacquainted, or but little acquainted with the Dravidian languages. No person who has any acquaintance with the principles of comparative philology, and who has carefully studied the grammars and vocabularies of the Dravidian languages, and compared them with those of Sanskrit, can suppose the grammatical structure and inflexional forms of those languages and the greater number of their more important roots, capable of being derived from Sanskrit by any process of development or corruption whatever." Much more might be said and many more arguments adduced to prove that the Dravidian languages are Scythian in their origin. But this has been done so thoroughly and successfully by Dr. Caldwell that we may safely accept his conclusion that Telugu is of Scythian origin—or at all events, that it is not Sanskrit. But whatever its origin may be, Telugu has certainly as-

B

sumed a Sanskrit dress.   There is scarcely a book of any
note that was not originally written in Sanskrit and translated into Telugu.   Telugu pundits delight in imitating
the Sanskrit, and are reluctant to admit that it is not an
offshoot of Sanskrit.

The Telugus are the most numerous of the Dravidian
races. Their number, however, has been greatly exagger-
ated by some, and unduly lessened by others.   This may
be accounted for in two ways: (1) By a loose use of the
word Telugus.   If we were to include all who live in the
Telugu country, as some have done, the number might
be put at eighteen or twenty millions.   But this would include for example a large number of Mohammedans, who
are almost as distinct in race and religion as Hindus and
Americans.   (2) It has been almost impossible to get at
the exact or even approximate number of Telugus in the
Nizam's dominions owing to a very defective system of
taking the census of that country.   At best it has been a
guess, and accordingly the estimated number of Telugus
has ranged between fourteen and twenty millions.   According to the census of 1891, the number of Telugus in
the Madras Presidency—that is, the number who gave
Telugu as their mother tongue, was—

Telugu country, Madras Presidency. . . . 11,754,946
The Nizam's Dominions. 4,279,108
Mysore   637,230
Scattering in Burma and elsewhere. . . .   332,074
Total. . . . 17,003,358

The Telugus are not now and never have been a migratory people, and hence it is not quite correct to say as has been said that "they are to be met with in all parts of Hindustan," if by that is meant more than is implied by the remark that "Americans are to be found in all parts of the world." It is true that in Madras there are nearly one hundred thousand Telugus; but though Madras is a Tamil city, it is but twenty-five miles from the Telugu country, and is the capital of the presidency, and naturally draws Telugus for the purpose of trade, for which they have a natural liking and fitness. A very large percentage of the native tradesmen of Madras are Telugus.

Besides Madras and Mysore, the only settlements that resemble a Telugu colony are those found in British Burma, chiefly in Rangoon and Moulmein. Dr. Stevens, of Rangoon, says: "In the ancient times when the Telugus were subject to their own rajahs or kings, the more enterprising of them appear to have ventured across the Bay of Bengal and established trading stations on the coast of Pegu and the Tenasserim province. They must have exerted a civilizing influence over the barbarians with whom they traded, for from the Telugus the ancestors of the Peguans obtained their written characters. To the most casual observer the general similarity in the shape of the letters and the vowel sounds of the two languages is quite striking. Combinations of circles and parts of circles are characteristic of both. Indeed, it seems probable that the term Taleing, by which the Burmese designate the Peguan, is derived from Telinga. The progenitors of the Burmese nation moving down the Irawadi valley toward the sea, discovered a people more civilized than themselves possessing books. To the mixed population of Peguans and black foreigners of the Telugu kingdom they appear to have given one common designation of Telinga or Taleing. From the Taleings the Burmese derived their alphabet, and with some modifications, their system of spelling. It will be seen then that the Burmese owe to the Telugus the first impulse which brought them up from a state of barbarism to the position which they now occupy among the half-civilized nations of the earth. The books which the different tribes in Burma are reading to-day, whether written with a stylus upon palm-leaf in some Buddhist monastery, or printed upon foreign paper on the mission press, may all be traced back more or less directly to ancient Telingana."

The religion of the Telugus is Hinduism, a corrupt form of Vedism. Vedism was the earliest form of religion of the great Indo-Aryan family. Their scriptures or sacred writings were contained in the Vedas, written as they claimed by inspired men called Rishis. The Vedas are a collection of songs, invocations, and prayers. These were addressed to natural objects, such as the wind, the sun, fire, and rain, as divine objects, but sometimes all were united into the one word God.

Brahmanism followed Vedism. It united all the forces of nature into a personal being called Brahma. Brahma was the only self-existent being; all else were but manifestations of the one great Spirit. The Brahmans added to the Vedas a sacrificial system of worship, and embodied it in a series of sacred writings called the Puranas, which were a ritual to guide the priests in their services, and also the history of their wars.

One of the most important developments of Brahmanism was the belief in a future state, and that rewards and punishments in the next world awaited all men according to their conduct in this. But perhaps the most remarkable idea in the whole system was that the gods were only mortals till by sacrifices and austerities they merited and obtained immortality from the Supreme Being. Men seeking merit and immortality followed the same course. The more valuable the sacrifice the greater the merit; hence human sacrifices became a part of the system.

The next addition to the sacred writings was the "Laws of Manu." We say sacred not because they relate exclusively to religion. Almost all distinctively Hindu books are sacred, though they treat of subjects purely secular. Thus the Mahabharata, which is sometimes called the Fifth Veda, is held to be most sacred, though it is simply a poetical history of the wars of the Kurus and Pandas—two races of rival kings. The laws of Manu elaborated and codified the laws of caste. They profess to be a commentary on the Vedas, but they are more than that. There is no caste in the Vedas, and the merest intimation of it in the Puranas; but in the laws of Manu it is fully developed. Hinduism grew out of Brahmanism. It was as Monier Williams says, "Brahmanism gone to seed and spread out into a confused tangle of divine personalities and incarnations." Besides, Brahma the creator, Vishnu the preserver, and Siva the destroyer, the later Puranas enumerate no less than three hundred and thirty millions of Hindu divinities. Though they are not regarded as equal to Brahma, Vishnu, and Siva, yet they are all worshiped as gods, so that the gods of the Hindus are more numerous than the Hindus themselves.

Idol worship was not at first a part of the Hindu system, and even now the educated Hindu *says* he does not worship the idol, but simply uses it as the medium through which he approaches the one living and true God. Some go even farther and say that the idol is nothing, and never was intended for *them*, but for the ignorant who could have no idea of God unless he were visible. But let any one go to a Hindu temple at the time of worship, and especially at a festival, and whom does he see, the ignorant, that is, the low and uneducated only ? Nay, verily ! high and low, rich and poor, educated and uneducated are there to worship their particular divinity Perhaps, in a few cases, God may be the object of worship, but in the vast majority of cases they are there to worship simply the idol, with no thought of a higher god. India is full of idols. Every village, however insignificant, has its temple, and in cities they can be counted by hundreds. Besides the public temples every house has its shrine and household gods.

The Telugus in common with all other Hindus tenaciously adhere to caste. If Hindu caste were simply a social institution, little could be said against it. Such a caste is common to all countries, even to democratic America. But Hindu caste is altogether a different institution from the social class distinctions of other countries. It is to-day, and has been for more than two thousand years, essentially a religious institution. Its fundamental idea is that God created distinct classes of men, and that it is utterly impossible to change this divine order. A Brahman is born a Brahman, and be he never so base he can by no possibility cease to be a Brahman so long as he observes the laws of his caste. In like manner a Sudra, be he never so learned, virtuous, and benevolent, can by no possibility ever rise to a higher caste. He was born or created by God a servant, and a servant he must forever remain.

At first there were but four castes: (1) the Brahmans or priests; (2) the Kshetryas or warriors; (3) the Vysias or farmers and traders; (4) The Sudras or servants. But besides these there have grown up from time to time innumerable castes, sometimes called trade castes, according to the various occupations which have come into existence as the demand for them came into being. Every trade and branch of industry has its particular caste, and no member of them ever dreams of following any other calling than that in which he was born.

That is the theory or law of caste, but the practice is somewhat different. Only the Brahmans and, to some extent, the Kshetryas have maintained their purity of caste. The Sudras of to-day occupy a very different position from that assigned them by the laws of Manu. They are no longer the menial servants of the Brahmans. They are now to a large extent the owners of the soil. The Reddis, who are a sub-class of the Sudras, are recognized as high caste, and are in fact the backbone of the country, being its chief cultivators. As a class they are still illiterate, though slowly but surely they are rising in the intellectual and social scale.

Even the Pariahs or out-castes occupy a very different position to-day from that which they held a century or less ago. Manu said respecting them : " Their abode must be out of town ; their clothes must be the mantles

of the dead ; let no man hold any intercourse with them."
Western civilization has done much to change all this.
Formerly when a caste-man met a Pariah on the public
road the latter was obliged to jump into the hedge or
ditch to allow the high-caste man to pass uncontaminated.
But when railways were introduced, rather than pay
second or first-class fare, the caste-man took his place in a
third-class carriage with his Pariah brother. Formerly
no caste-man would receive from a Pariah's hands a letter
or a parcel, but it had to be placed on the floor at some
distance. Now caste and non-caste men mingle more or
less freely in government offices.

When mission schools were opened to caste Hindus, as
well as Christians and Pariahs, the Brahmans scorned the
idea of sitting on the same bench with a Pariah or Christian. But as the success of mission schools did not depend on Brahmans, they could afford to dispense with
their presence. But not so easily could the Brahmans
dispense with an education. Now all classes alike sit side
by side without remonstrance.

But notwithstanding all these innovations, caste is still
a most powerful factor in the Hindu system, and is of all
others the most formidable obstacle to the spread of civilization and Christianity in India. To break caste is the
very last thing a Hindu is willing to do ; it is the climax
of all self-denial. Rather than take food or water from
the hands of a low-caste man or Christian, many Hindus
would prefer to die. No stronger proof can be given of
a man's conversion than his willingness to break his caste.
Even after his conversion the probabilities are that his
innate caste prejudices will keep cropping out. We sel-

dom, if ever, find a Christian from the Mala class select-
ing for a wife a girl from the Madigas, although, strictly
speaking, both of these classes belong to the out-castes.

There are not wanting many and striking indications
that caste is losing its hold upon the people, but its com-
plete destruction will not be seen in this generation or
the next. It will be a slow process, but it must come,
and when it does, Hinduism will be no more.

CHAPTER II.

ORIGIN OF THE MISSION.

Mr. Day's and Mr. Abbott's work contrasted. Mission of the London Missionary Society among the Telugus. Preparation of the Scriptures. The mission at Vizagapatam. Coming of Mr. Day. Establishment of a mission at Chicacole. Removal to Madras. Formation of an English Baptist church. Mr. Day's removal to Nellore. Difficulties of the transfer. Route finally chosen. Completion of canal and railroad facilities.

IT was a strange providence that gave to the Rev. Samuel S. Day the undivided honor of being the founder of the Telugu Mission. With him had been associated the Rev. E. L. Abbott. Both were appointed by the Baptist Board as missionaries to the Telugus, September, 20, 1835. Together they sailed from Boston in the ship "Louvre," September 22, 1835, and arrived in Calcutta, February 5, 1836. The Rev. Howard Malcom accompanied them as a deputation from the Baptists of America to visit our Asiatic Missions. When they reached Calcutta it was decided that Mr Abbott should not go to the Telugus, but to the Karens of Burma instead.

Very different was the reception these two servants of Christ were to meet in their respective fields. Abbott went to a field already prepared to receive "the white book" and "the white teacher." The people were in a state of expectancy. When they heard of the white man's arrival many of them went long distances to find him and see the white book.

Not so did the Telugus wait for Mr. Day. The mis-

REV. SAMUEL S. DAY.

sionary had to make long journeys through an enemy's country to find those who were even willing to hear the good news he had brought to them.

The London Missionary Society was the first to establish a Protestant mission among the Telugus. As this has frequently been described as "a feeble effort, which was attended with little or no success, and was eventually relinquished," a brief account of it may be interesting. The labors of our own missionaries will be better understood, and possibly better appreciated, when we know what had been done and some of the difficulties that had been encountered and overcome by those who preceded them.

The mission was commenced in 1805 by two missionaries who had been sent out to the Tamils of Tranquebar; but after a few months it was deemed expedient for them to undertake mission work in some part of India where Christ had not been named. Their attention was directed to the Telugus by a gentleman in the government service, who thus wrote of one of the difficulties they would have to meet: "I am sorry it is not in my power at present to furnish you with any elementary books to facilitate your acquisition of this fine dialect. There is, however, a manuscript rudimental grammar to be procured, which may be of use."

Notwithstanding the great scarcity of books, the language was acquired, and in 1818 a version of the New Testament was prepared and published. How far the translators were aided by the translation of Dr. Carey it is impossible to say. The Old Testament was also roughly translated, though not published until some years later. This was, probably, entirely their own work.

From 1832 to 1835 there was no missionary at Vizagapatam, and this probably accounts for the impression that the mission was "relinquished." The condition of the mission at this time seems to have been like that of our own from 1846 to 1849, with this difference, that while our Board seriously discussed the question of abandoning Nellore, we have no intimation that such a question had ever been raised by the London Mission respecting Vizagapatam.

In 1835, the Rev. J. W. Gordon, son of a former missionary, arrived in Vizagapatam. Several conversions took place that year. Thirteen schools were maintained in and about Vizagapatam. The Rev. E. Porter joined the mission that year, and Mrs. Gordon and Mrs. Porter had a girls' boarding school of from eighty to one hundred native girls. In 1836, the first Protestant chapel among the Telugus was built. The Sunday-school numbered one hundred and fifty. A press was set up from which were issued a revised version of the New Testament and portions of the Old Testament above referred to; also twenty thousand tracts, averaging five pages each, were issued annually, besides elementary school-books, Pilgrim's Progress, Peep of Day, etc., all prepared by the missionaries of Vizagapatam.

This was the condition of the London Mission when Mr. Day landed at Vizagapatam, March 7, 1836. The new missionaries were kindly received by the Rev. and Mrs. J. W. Gordon, of the London Mission. Mr. Day preached frequently for Mr. Gordon, and in other ways assisted him all he could. But he wanted to be in some place where he could begin a mission of his own ; hence after a few months he and Mrs. Day removed to Chicacole, about seventy miles north of Vizagapatam. Here they commenced the study of Telugu and attempted some work. Although a fair beginning had been made, Mr. Day did not feel satisfied that it was the place for the permanent mission. In consultation with Mr. Malcom it was decided to remove the mission to Madras, to which city he and Mrs. Day proceeded, arriving there March 7, 1837, exactly one year from the date of his arrival at Vizagapatam.

Here he spent three years, preaching both in English and Telugu. On the 4th of August, 1838, an English Baptist church was organized under the leadership of Mr. Day, who became its acting pastor. It consisted of fifteen members, some of whom had been converted and were members of our churches in Moulmein and Tavoy, Burma The Confession of Faith adopted was that known as the " Danville Articles," or Articles of the Danville, Vt., Association.

During the three years Mr. Day resided in Madras he made repeated and extensive tours up into the Telugu country. He found that between Madras and Vizagapatam, a distance of nearly four hundred miles, and a territory containing at least ten millions of people, there was not a single missionary. Moreover, while he had met with some success in his English work, he had thus far not baptized a single Telugu convert. He therefore resolved that as he had been appointed a missionary to the Telugus, he should be where the Telugus chiefly were.

Hence, on the 9th of February, 1840, he announced to
the church in Madras that he had decided to remove to
Nellore, and accordingly resigned his office as pastor.

Although the distance from Madras to Nellore is only
a hundred and eight miles, the journey in those days, especially with a family of small children, was a considerable undertaking.   Mr. Day had the choice cf two routes.
First there was the great Northern Trunk Road which
connects Madras and Secunderabad and passes through
Nellore and Ongole.   To make the journey by this road
would require five or six carts drawn by bullocks, and occupy six nights, stopping during the day at rest houses or
bungalows along the way to avoid the heat and to rest
and feed both passengers and bullocks.   The other route,
and the one Mr. Day selected, was by canal to Sulurpett,
which was at that time the limit of what is now known as
the Buckingham Canal, named after the Duke of Buckingham because completed under his administration as
governor during the famine.   Mr. Day provided two
rude native boats for himself, family, and effects, and
started in the evening making the journey to Sulurpett in
two nights and one day.   That was the easiest part of the
journey.   From Sulurpett to Nellore is sixty miles, and
over the rough road between the two, Mrs. Day and two
children were carried in a palanquin ; little Malcom and
his ayah (nurse) in a dooly—a sort of extempore palanquin—and the rest in country carts.   Thus they reached
Nellore in about the same time that would have been required had they gone by road, but with much less fatigue.

The facilities of travel between Madras and Nellore
were somewhat improved by the completion of the Buck-

ingham Canal both with respect to time and comfort. The canal reaches within sixteen miles of Nellore, and the style of boats has been much improved, so that the journey can now be made with comfort in forty-eight hours, or less if the wind is favorable. The boats can only sail when t' e wind is fair; otherwise they are drawn by coolies on the bank or poled along in the lakes and back-waters

There is now a railway which connects Nellore with the Madras and Bombay Railway, and gives it railroad communication with all the principal cities of India. There are also two other lines of railroad under construction, and a third is projected which when finished will connect almost every station in the mission with every other. So that the day is not distant when the whole system of missionary itinerancy in this mission will be completely revolutionized.

CHAPTER III.

NELLORE is the chief city of the Nellore District.
As this word "district" will frequently occur in
these pages, it may as well be explained that the presidency of Madras is divided into twenty-two districts, each
of which is governed by an English official called the
collector. Besides being the collector of revenue, he is
the chief magistrate of the district. His position hardly
corresponds to that of the governor of a State, and yet it is
nearer to that than anything else in our home government.
His salary is one thousand two hundred pounds a year.
The judge of the district occupies the same official rank,
and receives the same pay, but his duties are exclusively
confined to the court. Besides these, there are other English officials, such as the surgeon, the district engineer,
superintendent of police, etc., and an almost endless
number of native subordinates. The Nellore District is
one hundred and seventy miles long from north to south,
and seventy miles wide from east to west, and contains

eight thousand seven hundred and fifty-one square miles of territory, and about one and one-fourth millions of people.

Nellore town or city, for it is a municipality, is one hundred and seven miles north of Madras and sixteen miles inland from the sea. It is situated on the south bank of the river Pennar, and contains very nearly thirty thousand people. The name Nellore, like so many other Telugu names, had its origin in a legend. There is said to have been a chief called Mukkanti Reddi who had large herds. Among them, there was a cow into which the soul of a Brahman woman was supposed to have passed. This cow had a revelation that Siva had appeared on earth in the form of a lingam. This stone was situated under a tree called the Nelli-chettu (philanthus emblica). The cow was observed to resort daily to the stone and bedew it with its milk. For this the cowherd struck the cow, whereupon blood flowed from it. Mukkanti, who had had a vision, was directed to erect a temple on the spot, which he accordingly did. The adjoining village received the name Nelli-uru, from nelli the name of the tree, and uru a village, hence Nelluru or Nellore. Nellore was formerly surrounded by a rampart wall, and had a fort of considerable importance; but only portions of the wall can now be seen, and the fort is dilapidated, though still used for government offices.

Mr. Day and family left Madras, February 18th, and arrived in Nellore, February 26, 1840. He was soon afterward followed by the Rev. S. Van Husen and wife, who had been appointed to the Telugus, and sailed from Boston, October 22, 1839, arriving in Madras in March,

1840.   Mr. Day at first rented a small bungalow, but with the aid of Judge Walker, who became a warm friend of the mission, he obtained a grant from government of eight acres of land for a mission compound.   On this compound, the present bungalow or mission house was erected in 1841, and soon after a small chapel directly in front of it and close to the road.

If we may judge from the size of the bungalow and the solid manner in which it was built, we should say that Mr. Day must have had a decided conviction that he had at last found a place where he meant to stay, or at least where the mission was destined to stay.   How far Mr. Day's faith reached into the future we cannot say, but there are many evidences that he saw by faith what we have since beheld with the natural eye.

During the erection of the bungalow, an incident occurred which shows the gross superstition of the people at that time, and the progress that has been made in dispelling their darkness.   The foot-path between two of the pettas or hamlets of Nellore lay directly through what is now the mission compound.   The native who superintended the work, had been much annoyed by the constant passing and repassing of the people.   To get rid of them, he secretly informed a few that the missionary, in order to make his building more secure, intended capturing a lot of the children, and having cut off their heads, and offering them in sacrifice to his God, would bury them in the deep holes (foundations) he was digging.   This not only had the desired effect, but it so terrified the whole community that for many months Mr. Day had the greatest difficulty to persuade the people of the utter

MISSION BUNGALOW, NELLORE.

groundlessness of the story. But the gentle spirit and unmistakable love for the natives which so marked Mr. Day's character could not be resisted, and in time all traces of distrust died away. If such a story were started to-day, there is not a cooly in the whole region around who would give it the slightest credence.

Another evidence of progress is seen in the different treatment missionaries of to-day receive from that which sometimes greeted our pioneers. About seven miles west of Nellore there is a celebrated temple built on the summit of a hill called Nursimhakonda. To this temple's festival thousands of people resort once a year. With a view to teaching the vast crowds a better way, Mr. Day and a few native helpers went to the festival. In a village at the foot of the hill, called Zonnavada, a Brahman, becoming enraged at the preaching, deliberately took off his shoe and struck Mr. Day repeated blows on the head and face. Mr. Day had no disposition to prosecute the man, but the case reached the magistrate, who insisted upon bringing him to trial. The difficulty, however, of convicting a Brahman of crime was so great that he would no doubt have gotten off but for an eccentric native official, who stepped into the court uncalled and testified that he *saw* the prisoner beat Mr. Day. The Brahman was accordingly convicted, and fined five hundred rupees. Such a case as this is quite unheard of in this part of India now, though, as we shall see, similar cases occurred in other parts of the mission much later than Mr. Day's time.

Toward sunset on the 27th of September, 1841, a little company might have been seen wending its way toward the Pennar river. Right under the shadow of the great

Nellore temple on the river bank, they sang a hymn ; the
missionary read a few passages of Scripture, and explained
the nature of the ordinance about to be celebrated.   By
this time a large crowd of natives had assembled, and Mr.
Day embraced the opportunity to preach to them of Jesus
and the great salvation.   A brief prayer was then offered
and Venkappah, the first Telugu convert, was led down
into the river and baptized into the name of the Father,
Son, and Holy Ghost.   It was a strange sight to the won-
dering multitude, but a happy experience to Venkappah,
and probably one of the most blessed privileges of Mr.
Day's life.

About this time an old man from Ongole came to Nellore on business, and hearing that missionaries were there
called to see them.   He said that almost two years before,
he began to examine the Christian religion, and that he
was satisfied of its truth, and believed in Jesus Christ for
salvation.   He admitted that all should openly profess
Christ before men; "but," said he, "Ongole is a large
place ; there are no missionaries, no disciples of. Jesus
Christ there ; what can I do?"   He was supplied with
portions of the Scriptures and some tracts, and went back
to his family, followed by earnest prayer.   The next year
Mr. Van Husen visited Ongole and found this old man.
He was in the habit of praying and reading the Scriptures to his family and others.   His wives at first opposed
him, but afterward listened quietly.   This old man was a
Sudra, and although never baptized, he was in the habit
of preaching the new religion among the people of Ongole.   By whom he was led to the truth we do not know,
but it is probable that Venkappah, the first convert, who

lived beyond Ongole, had frequent conversations with him. Thus early in its history the influence of the mission had reached out into those regions that have since become so fruitful and famous.

The attendants in the schools in Nellore made good progress in learning the Scriptures. The native assistants were earnest and faithful, and though embarrassed by sickness, the missionaries were encouraged. "Yet we are grieved and disappointed," wrote Mr. Day, " because the interest felt by our denomination in the missionary cause is not such as to enable the Board to send any more missionaries here."

The Nellore Church was organized October 12, 1844, composed of eight members, namely: Rev. S. S. Day, Mrs. Day, Rev. S. Van Husen, Mrs. Van Husen, Elizabeth Jackson, Christian Nursu, J. Cay and Elisha. As in the church in Madras, the Confession of Faith adopted was the "Danville Articles."

At this time Mr. Van Husen was in a very precarious state of health. For a time he removed to Madras for change and better medical treatment, but instead of improving, his symptoms became more alarming. Nothing short of a return to America was likely to be of any avail, and even with this his recovery was extremely doubtful. Hence it was decided that he should go home. On Sunday, April 20, 1845, letters of dismission were granted to Mr. and Mrs. Van Husen, and in the evening Mr. Van Husen administered the Lord's Supper and bade farewell to the little church. They left Nellore the same week never again to return. The parting was painful to all, but especially so to Mr. Day, who was thus left alone, and that at

too, in very feeble health.   He wrote home most earnest
and touching appeals for help, but no help came.   At this
time cholera broke out in Nellore, so that the schools had
to be closed.   The following year (1846) Mr. Day's
health had so far declined that his physicians ordered his
immediate return to America.   " The thought of visiting
our native land," he said, " gives little satisfaction.   Oh !
the mission we leave—the little church—the few inquirers—the schools—the heathen—yes, the hundred thousand
heathen immediately in our vicinity—the million in the
district—the ten millions in our mission field—what will
become of them ? "

The necessity of spending so much money in taking
missionaries *from* the field rather than bringing men *to* it,
or of supporting them while *in* it, was very painful to Mr.
Day, and God mitigated the pain in his own case by raising up friends for him in Nellore and Madras, who provided the entire amount for the passage of himself and
family to the United States.

The mission was left in the care of two Eurasians, who
had done good service while the missionary remained, and
seemed to be trustworthy.   But it proved far otherwise.
As soon as the missionary had departed they entered upon
a most reckless career.   The schools were disbanded, the
church was scattered, and the mission bungalow, consecrated by the prayers and lives of devoted men of God, became the scene of drunken revels and shameless debauch.

It is, perhaps, well that this state of affairs was not
known to the Missionary Union in 1848, when the question was discussed at the annual meeting of that year,
whether the mission should be continued or abandoned.

History of the Telugu Mission.   Page 39.

REV. LYMAN JEWETT.

Had it been known, their decision to reinforce it might have been reversed. But that was not God's plan. His plan was to save the Telugus, and hence he put it into the hearts of his people to continue the mission.

It is said that the darkest hour of the twenty-four is that one just before day-break. The year 1848 was doubtless the darkest in the history of this mission. Nothing could appear more utterly hopeless, if its real state could have been known, than the condition of the mission at this time. But it was in that year that God put it into the heart of Lyman Jewett to consecrate his life to his service among the Telugus. That was at least the beginning of the dawn, as we shall see by-and-by.

Mr. Day's health having in some measure been restored, he left his family at home, and again sailed for India on the 10th of October, 1848, in the ship "Bowditch" from Boston. He was accompanied by the Rev. Lyman Jewett and wife. During the voyage, the captain was converted and many of the seamen were seriously impressed by the preaching, conversation, and lives of the missionaries.

On their arrival in Nellore, Mr. Day was shocked at the sad havoc Satan had made among the little flock. Almost every trace of his former work had been obliterated. But he had not lost his faith in God, nor yet in the work he had sent him to do. Hence he did not falter, but bravely sought to "rebuild the waste places." He resumed the chapel services on the 26th of March, 1849. His text was: "For I determined not to know anything among you, save Jesus Christ, and him crucified." He found he had not forgotten his Telugu, but had much freedom in preaching. There were some indications that serious impressions had been made on some of his hearers. Mr. and Mrs. Jewett were present, and in the evening meeting Mr. Jewett prayed most fervently for a blessing on the preached word.

Mr. and Mrs. Jewett made rapid progress in acquiring the Telugu, so that Mr. Jewett is said to have preached his first Telugu sermon in nine months after his arrival. Mrs. Jewett's command of the colloquial Telugu was remarkable. She early became interested in a girls' boarding school. Such a school had existed in Mrs. Day's time, but it had been scattered. They began the school with two or three little girls, one of whom was " Julia," now so well known, and two or three little orphan boys. Mr. Day was deeply interested in the children. He watched over them as he would his own, and frequently performed such acts of menial service for them as few fathers would care to do even for their own children. He taught them daily in the school, prayed with them, and in every way tried to lead them to the Saviour.

" Julia " was the first fruits of this school, and if there had never been another convert, she alone would be ample compensation for all it has cost. But Julia was not secured without a struggle, not with her, but on account of her with her heathen mother. A deep religious spirit pervaded the little company of believers, and the Spirit of the Lord seemed to be with them. Julia evidently was much impressed and expressed an earnest wish to be baptized. Her mother also appeared to be inquiring, and Julia had no fears about getting her mother's consent to her being baptized. But when the request was made, she seemed to be possessed. She came to the missionaries and

History of the Telugu Mission.   Page 40.
JULIA OF NELLORE.

demanded her child. She would listen to no argument or reason. She professed to be sick and needed her daughter to wait on her. She wept and wailed until Julia overcome by a sense of duty to her mother joined in her request to be allowed to go. So she had to be given up, but it was only for a time.

On the 28th of March, 1852, Julia and Mrs. Gilmore, the matron of the school, were baptized by Mr. Jewett in the great tank or lake in Nellore. These were the first converts Mr. Jewett baptized, and it was a happy day for the missionaries and the little company of native believers. Julia says of that event: "It was truly a happy day for me! The sun was just rising, and everything was so beautiful. Father Day led me out into the lake and Father Jewett baptized me. I have had many afflictions since then, but I have never lost the sweet comfort I then found in following my precious Saviour."

Besides the boarding school, Mr. Day had opened several day schools in which English as well as Telugu was taught. The chief portion of the time was given to the Bible, and the reading books were prepared on Christian principles. So that in these schools, some two hundred and seventy were receiving a thoroughly Christian education from which the missionaries looked for much precious results. Hence, it was a sore bereavement to Mr. Day when he received from the Executive Committee an order that all such schools should be closed, and no appropriations for such work would be made for the year beginning October 1, 1850. There was no alternative but to obey and close the schools.

Mr. Day was a pronounced evangelistic missionary.

He had no idea of educating people into the kingdom of God. At the same time he regarded schools with great favor even as an evangelistic agency. Hence, he felt that this order was as a severe blow to the mission. The present policy of the mission in regard to schools is not very different from that which Mr. Day appears to have held forty years ago. But it does not follow that our present school system would have been a wise one then. Circumstances are very different. Though we admit heathen children to our schools, and hope for and even expect their conversion, yet our primary object in opening schools, is for the education of our Christian youth.

On the spot now occupied by the girls' school there used to be a small Hindu temple, which was a source of great annoyance to the mission. Mr. Day had made frequent attempts to get it removed, but in vain. But at last the old priest died, and as his children could not carry on the work of deception which brought the old man so much gain, they decided to sell it, or rather the land it stood on. Funds were collected, the old temple was purchased and removed, and in its stead a small building for the boarding school was erected. It cost some seven hundred rupees, most of which was given by the friends in Nellore. This served the purpose till 1876, when it gave place to the present building.

In January, 1851, Mr. Day made a tour to the west as far as Udayagiri. At Sungam, twenty miles west of Nellore, he met Mr. and Mrs. Jewett, and spent a delightful Sunday with them in worship and social intercourse. Leaving them to continue their work about Sungam, he proceeded to Atmakur. He had rather a difficult journey, as there were no such roads then as there are now.

His path lay across rice fields, along ridges scarcely wide enough for his pony to walk on, groping his way in the darkness, and every now and then stumbling into a ditch. Once his pony tumbled and threw him into the mud. Still he pushed on, and in due time arrived at Atmakur, glad enough to find his tent pitched and ready for him. After preaching in Atmakur, and the surrounding neighborhood, he continued his journey westward. At the next halting place he entered a village called Karatampaud to preach. But he was immediately ordered out. He protested and remonstrated, but the people would listen to no reason, and out he was actually driven. This was quite illegal, and Mr. Day might have had the villagers punished, but that was not his way. When, however, they got outside the village and on the highway, Mr. Day refused to be driven any farther, and there he preached to the crowd that had gathered.

After spending ten days on the top of Udayagiri Droog (a fortified hill), they came down and resumed their work of preaching and distributing tracts and Scripture portions. On leaving Udayagiri, Mr. Day exclaimed: "Oh, for a couple of mission families to live somewhere in this region, and to labor among this people!" If it is permitted the redeemed to look down upon the scenes of their former labors, Mr. Day now sees that wish literally fulfilled, for since 1884, Mr. and Mrs. Burditt have faithfully labored at Udayagiri, and Mr. and Mrs. Stone are stationed at Atmakur.

In the three years that had now passed since the arrival

of the missionaries, notwithstanding many discouragements, a very hopeful impetus had been given to the work. The number of converts, it is true, had been very few as yet, still there were indications of greater prosperity. But in January, 1853, a second deputation, consisting of Messrs. Peck and Granger, visited Nellore. They found the missionaries laboring faithfully and hopefully ; but as the conversions had been so few, and as Mr. Day's health was again in a very precarious condition, the report carried home was not very inspiring.

CHAPTER IV.

THE LONE STAR.

Another crisis for the mission. Resolution of the Board to close it. "The Lone Star." Effect on the Missionary Union. The question at Nellore. Mr. Day again laid aside. Mr. Jewett at Ongole. Prayer-meeting hill. The missionary's prediction verified. Accession of Mr. and Mrs. Douglass to the mission. Two converts—Canakiah and Lydia. "Anna the Prophetess." An appeal for additional help. Mr. Jewett's remonstrance. The death of Nursu. The schools of the mission. Paying children to attend. The Indian mutiny. Purchase of property at Ongole. Failure of Mr. Jewett's health. The work of Mr. Douglass. Native evangelists. Suspension of their work, and departure of Mr. Douglass.

THE year 1853 will ever be memorable in the history of the mission, owing to two very remarkable events, one of which occurred at home, the other at Ongole. The annual meetings of the Missionary Union were held that year at Albany, N. Y. On account of the very indifferent success that had attended the Telugu Mission for seventeen years, the question came up for the second time, "Shall the mission be re-inforced or discontinued?" The Union naturally turned to the deputation just returned from Nellore, but they had nothing very definite or decisive to report. On the one hand, the field was wide and open; the missionaries had acquired the language, and a few converts had been made. But on the other hand, the progress made had been very small, and the field *could* be cared for by other societies laboring among the Telugus, though at some distance from the field occupied by our missionaries. Viewed in the light of the

45

Lord's commission, there was nothing which warranted a
retreat.

The question was referred to the Board, where a proposition was made that a lettter be written to Dr. Jewett
requesting him to close up the mission and remove to Burma.   Dr. Edward Bright, then acting corresponding
secretary, said, " And who will write the letter? and who
will write the letter? " intimating, by repeating the question and by the tone of his voice, that write it who might,
he certainly would not.

In the evening, when the question came up in the public
meeting for discussion, a number of very earnest and eloquent addresses were made.   One of the speakers, in the
course of his address, turned to the mission map which
hung on the wall, and pointing to Nellore, called it the
"Lone Star Mission," there being but the one station.
The Rev. S. F. Smith, D. D., author of our National
Hymn, caught up the words "lone star," and before he
slept wrote the following lines :

"THE LONE STAR."

Shine on, " Lone Star ! " Thy radiance bright
    Shall spread o'er all the eastern sky ;
Morn breaks apace from gloom and night :
    Shine on, and bless the pilgrim's eye.

Shine on, " Lone Star ! " I would not dim
    The light that gleams with dubious ray ;
The lonely star of Bethlehem
    Led on a bright and glorious day.

Shine on, " Lone Star ! " in grief and tears,
    And sad reverses oft baptized ;
Shine on amid thy sister spheres :
    Lone stars in heaven are not despised.

Shine on, " Lone Star !" Who lifts his hand
    To dash to earth so bright a gem,
A new " lost pleiad " from the band
    That sparkles in night's diadem?

Shine on, "Lone Star !" The day draws near
    When none shall shine more fair than thou ;
Thou, born and nursed in doubt and fear
    Wilt glitter on Immanuel's brow.

Shine on, " Lone Star !" till earth redeemed,
    In dust shall bid its idols fall ;
And thousands, where thy radiance beamed
    Shall " crown the Saviour, Lord of all."

When Dr. Smith came down to breakfast the next morning, he handed to his friend, Judge Harris, a slip of paper,
with the remark, " Those are my opinions of the Telugu
Mission." The judge read the little poem, but instead of
returning it, as Dr. Smith expected, he quietly appropiated
it, carried it to the meeting, and read the verses. Many
wept and sobbed during the reading, and whatever of
doubt remained as to continuing the mission was now removed. It was unanimously voted to reinforce the mission,
provided it could be done without prejudice to the Burman
Mission.

While these discussions were going on at home, a very
different state of things existed in Nellore. The question
of abandoning the mission never once entered the minds
of the missionaries. There was no doubting or wavering
with them. They might live or die, but the mission must
go on. On almost the very day when these discussions
were going on at Albany, the missionaries were re-organ-
izing the Nellore Church, after the defections that had
occurred in the absence of the missionaries. A number of

converts had been baptized, and were now added to the
church. Inquirers were multiplying and fresh hopes were
inspiring the little band of Christian laborers.

But in the midst of this flush of prosperity, God once
more sorely tested their faith by again laying aside from
active service the father of the mission. Mr. Day's health
broke down, and he was obliged, for the second time, to
quit the mission and the country, never again to return.
When in addition to this, the report reached Mr. Jewett
that it had been proposed to remove him to Burma, it had
a most depressing effect. He said, "I would rather labor
on here as long as I live than to be torn up by the roots
and transplanted. Faith and my own conscience tell me
that I am not laboring in vain in the Lord."

It was toward the close of 1853 that the other event to
which reference has been made took place. Mr. and Mrs.
Jewett, with a few native helpers, made a tour to the north
as far as Guntur. They reached Ongole the last week in
December, and spent five or six days preaching in the
streets. The people heard them, if not gladly, at least respectfully. There was no abuse, no violence, and above
all they were not "assailed with hootings and stones," as
has been reported. It had been a custom at the mission-
house in Nellore for some years to hold a prayer meeting
early on the first day of the new year. It was therefore
arranged that on this New Year's day (1854) they should
hold their prayer meeting on the top of the hill which over-
looks Ongole. Accordingly, at 4 o'clock in the morning,
Mr. and Mrs. Jewett, Christian Nursu, Julia, and Ruth
started from their tent, and climbed the hill. Julia says:
"I carried a stool, and Ruth carried a mat, and when we

reached the top of the hill we all sat down. First, we sung a hymn, and Father Jewett prayed; then Christian Nursu prayed; then father read a portion of Isaiah, fifty-second chapter, 'How beautiful upon the mountains are the feet of him that bringeth good tidings.' Then Mother Jewett prayed, then I prayed, and then Ruth prayed. When Father Jewett prayed, I remember he said, 'As the sun is now about to rise and shine upon the earth so may the sun of righteousness arise quickly and shine upon this dark land.' After we had all prayed, Father Jewett stood up, and stretching out his hand, said : 'Do you see that rising piece of ground yonder, all covered over with prickly pear? Would you not like that spot for our mission bungalow and all this land to become Christian? How would you like it? Well, Nursu, Julia, that day will come!' Then we all spoke our minds, and just as the meeting closed, the sun rose. It seemed as if the Holy Spirit had lifted us above the world, and our hearts were filled with thanksgiving to the Lord."

The first part of Dr. Jewett's prediction has been fulfilled to the letter, for it is on the very spot pointed out that Dr. Clough's house now stands. And this is the more remarkable, because it was not selected by the mission, but by a gentleman who built the house for himself, and afterward sold it to the mission. The second part of the prediction seems a long way off as yet, but scarcely more so than the first seemed at that time. But be it near or far, it is as sure to come as God's word is true. Thus, both at home and in the mission, an earnest faith in God's word and in the mission led its friends to predict with almost prophetic assurance a glorious future for the " Lone Star."

In October, 1854, the Rev. F. A. Douglass and wife sailed from Boston to join the mission. They reached Nellore early the following year. Mr. Douglass was a hard worker. He became exceedingly fond of the Telugu and acquired an exceptionally good command of the colloquial dialect. He made extensive tours into the district, and did much in scattering the good seed of the gospel. Among the few converts of this time there were two who deserve more than a passing notice. One was Canakiah, a schoolboy, who became the first ordained pastor of the mission ; the other was Lydia, whom Dr. Smith called " Anna the prophetess."

Canakiah was the son of a Sepoy belonging to the 17th Madras Light Infantry. He was born at Bangalore, in the native state of Mysore, in 1837, while the regiment was at that station. His parents belonged to the Naidu division of the Sudra caste. When about eight years old his father took his pension and was returning to his native place, Vizagapatam, but stopped at Nellore to visit a relative. This relative was a pensioned subahdar, an officer corresponding to sergeant, who had been converted while his regiment was at Moulmein, and was baptized by Dr. Haswell. While in Nellore, Canakiah's father died, and was buried in the mission burying ground. After his father's death he attended the mission school as a day scholar, but after Messrs. Day and Jewett arrived, in 1849, he was admitted into the boarding school.

Thus for a number of years he had been under Christian influence, and by the time he reached his eighteenth year he was fully convinced of his need of a Saviour, and of the truth of Christianity. He was baptized by Mr.

History of the Telugu Mission. Page 50.
REV. N. CANAKIAH, FIRST ORDAINED PASTOR.

Jewett, January 10, 1855. His rapid growth in grace and knowledge of the Scriptures, as well as his earnest life and the great scarcity of laborers, led the missionary to put him into the work while yet very young. At first he taught school, and occasionally went out with the missionary on his preaching tours. For this work he developed special qualifications, and hence was soon relieved of his school work, and devoted himself entirely to evangelistic work.

On the 20th of August, 1856, Canakiah was married to Julia, and on the 14th of December, 1861, he was ordained pastor of the Nellore Church, and thus became the first ordained native preacher of the mission. But this pastoral relation lasted only a few years, owing to the pressing need of evangelistic laborers and Canakiah's special qualifications for that work. Hence, soon after Mr. Jewett's arrival, in 1865, Canakiah was relieved of his pastoral duties and devoted himself to evangelistic labors, in which he has continued up to the present time.

As a Christian, Canakiah's record is clean. His honesty is absolutely above suspicion. No man in the mission has been trusted more, and certainly no man is more worthy of confidence. He is an able and eloquent preacher, and though his educational advantages have been limited, his general influence for good has probably never been surpassed by any of the native assistants.

Lydia was a woman of the Sudra caste, and lived at Vizagapatam at the time of her conversion, which took place in her forty-ninth year. Returning from one of the great Hindu festivals, Lydia's attention was directed to a house where a number of Christians were assembled. She

stopped, and they began to preach to her about Christ.
She became very angry and spoke rudely to the Christians. She tried to defend her religion, claiming that there
was no difference between their religion and hers. The
next day she went again to the Christians and heard them
read the Bible. Again she went away angry, but could
not banish from her mind the words she had heard. The
third day she went again, and with a similar result. A
fourth time she visited the Christians, but this time it
was not to dispute, but with the question " How can I obtain salvation ? " They told her she would understand
all if she only read the Bible. " But," she said, " I cannot read. Then they told me," she continued, " 'if I
prayed to God he would enlighten me.' I started from
there with much sorrow. Then I went to the seashore
and got some sand, and next day went to the Christian's
house and laid down the sand, and asked the Christians
to teach me my letters, and by-and-by I would be able to
read the Bible." In a very few months Lydia had
learned to read. Her caste people discovered her secret,
and would have made trouble for her, but they feared the
disgrace they themselves would fall into if they exposed
the fact that one of their caste-women had learned to read
the Bible.

Although fully convinced of the truth of Christianity,
and in all probability truly converted, Lydia tried to be
a secret Christian, and did not dare attend a Christian
church, much less be baptized. But the Lord both
opened her eyes and prepared the way for her to confess
Christ. Her people removed to Nellore, and though they
urged her to come, she refused and stayed in Vizagapa-

tam. She then began to attend the chapel of the London
Mission, and four months afterward she was baptized.
Six months after her baptism she went to Nellore, and instead of going to her relatives she went to the mission compound and asked for a place to stay. Here she remained
four years, worshiping and laboring with the Christians,
but without uniting with the church. At the end of this
time, Mr. Jewett said to her: "Lydia, this is not right;
you ought to go back to the London Mission, where you
can enjoy the communion of the Lord's Supper." But
she refused to go, and said she wished to unite with
the church in Nellore. This course she accordingly
took.

From the day of her baptism, Lydia consecrated herself, body, soul, and all she possessed, to the service of
Christ. For more than thirty years she has been a devoted Christian and a faithful Bible woman. She has a
remarkably clear voice and distinct articulation, and in
her addresses holds an audience as few native women can.
But her chief characteristic is her passion for prayer and
her wonderful faith. It has been her custom for many
years to spend several hours each day in prayer before
going out to read and preach to her countrywomen. Except when prevented by sickness, her place at worship
and meetings for prayer is never vacant, and at the latter
she rarely fails to take her part.

Her general appearance, dress, and manner, together
with her remarkable utterances led Dr. S. F. Smith, when
in Nellore, to give her the name of "Anna the Prophetess." Lydia had long been familiar with the early struggles of the mission, and knew something of the origin of

Dr. Smith's "Lone Star." So one day, when Dr. and Mrs. Smith were sitting on the veranda of the bungalow, Lydia came and sat down at their feet. Taking them both by the knees, she said : "We have never seen Abraham and Sarah, but we see you." By which she meant to say that the next best thing to seeing Abraham and Sarah was to see Dr. Smith and his wife, who had interceded for the Telugus, and had predicted with almost prophetic assurance the glorious things that had since then come to pass.

Lydia is now very feeble and almost blind. It is only when she prays that she exhibits anything of her former vigor ; but in this she seems as much at home as ever. She says she is simply waiting for the call of God, and hoping to enter very soon into the presence of her Lord. Would that all were as certain of "an abundant entrance."

In 1855, the missionaries united in a most earnest appeal to the Executive Committee for additional help. In reply, the members of the Committee said that seldom, if ever, had they listened to an appeal that carried with it such force and conviction, yet at the same time they felt their utter inability to respond to it. Not only so, but they said that the expenditure must be still further reduced if there was not a large advance in the liberality of the churches.

To this Mr. Jewett replied in April, 1856. He deplored the condition of the churches at home that could tolerate the idea of retrenching their foreign mission work. "Oh, Father, forgive the churches!" he exclaimed. "To rob God's treasury is not to distress missionaries pecuniarily, but it is a robbery of souls—shutting

away eternally the gift of life. The missionary must part
with what he loves far more than any earthly boon, yet
Christians at home refuse the help they could so easily
give. The very idea of retrenchment is hostile to everything that deserves the name of missionary. Satan says:
'Stop giving;' Jesus says: 'Go ye into all the world and
preach the gospel.'"

In November of this year, the mission suffered a
grievous loss in the death of the faithful, devoted colporteur and preacher, Christian Nursu. In the room where
the writer now sits, a little company of Christians gathered around the dying Christian. Nursu assured them
that all was well, and although the monsoon storm raged
without, all was peace and calm within. "The same
truths," said Nursu, "that I have preached to others, are
now my joy and support." And thus in the triumph of
Christian faith his soul passed from earth to heaven.

The mission could ill afford to lose the service of so
valuable a helper; but to witness such a triumphant death
was worth all the sacrifices that had been made and labor
expended to secure it. It was an inspiration to those
who witnessed it. How many were saved by Nursu's
life no one can tell, but, by his death, at least one man
for whom he had earnestly labored was led to give himself to Christ.

By 1857, the boarding and day schools had made considerable progress. In the case of day scholars, the practice of paying the parents a small sum of money to induce
them to send their children to school, was still in vogue.
In our day this would be regarded as a very doubtful
policy, and it is a question whether it ever was, on the

whole, a wise one. The reasons for adopting it were first, the extreme poverty of the people, requiring them to put their children out to work as soon as they could earn two or three farthings a day at cooly work ; second, their total ignorance of the value of education ; and third, the desire of the missionaries to impress the children with the truths of Christianity. On the other hand, it may well be questioned whether this practice did not foster the conviction, almost universal among the natives, that anything and everything done to gratify the missionary ought to be paid for. That the mission treasury might not be charged with this expense, a "Juvenile Benevolent Society" was organized. The children were taught to sew and make their own clothes. A sale of the articles made was held and a considerable sum realized. Still, the money paid to the parents came from the missionary, and it mattered not to them where nor how the missionary got it. But whether the practice was wise or otherwise, it has long since been abandoned.

Early in this year (1857), Mr. Douglass and family removed to Madras owing to the ill health of Mrs. Douglass. This was the year of the terrible Sepoy mutiny, and although Nellore was far remote from the scene of actual war, yet all India was more or less disturbed, at least by rumors of impending danger. Hence, acting on the advice of friends, Mr. Jewett and family also removed to Madras in August and remained till January, 1858, when both missionaries returned to Nellore. Thirteen were baptized that year, the largest number yet received in any one year.

The death of Jacob, a faithful and efficient helper, and

a number of exclusions from the church, caused much
sorrow. But these reverses were followed by a precious
work of grace, and the baptism of six converts. Among
them was a girl named Maha-Lukshumammah, who afterward became the wife of Rungiah, now the head assistant
of the missionary in Perambore, Madras.

In 1860, Mr. and Mrs. Jewett, their daughters Addie
and Hattie, and Canakiah spent three months in Ongole,
from January to April. It was at this time that Mr.
Jewett negotiated for the house and land which became
the mission bungalow and compound. He did not know
where the money was to come from, nor who would occupy
the house, but he believed that the prediction he had
made in 1854, on the hill top, would be fulfilled, and
that God would send the money and the man too. So
the house was bought, and Mr. Jewett, after asking the
money from the Lord, wrote to a friend and classmate at
home about the matter. When the letter was received,
the friend had just been considering what to do with a
sum he wished to invest in the Lord's work. He immediately sent it to Mr. Jewett, and it was just sufficient to
purchase the house and land, and make some necessary
repairs.

It was also during this stay at Ongole that Mr. Jewett
baptized the first convert in Ongole. His name was
Obulu, who became and remained a faithful preacher till
his death, in 1880.

After thirteen years of earnest and faithful labor, in
what many regarded as a fruitless and almost hopeless
effort to establish a mission at Nellore, Mr. Jewett's health
broke down in 1862, and he and his family were obliged

to return home. Being obliged to relinquish his much-loved work was a great grief. He said: "The trial of leaving home in the first place was less than nothing compared with that of leaving the mission field to return."

Mr. Douglass was thus left alone in charge of the mission. He continued preaching in the chapel and in the streets of Nellore and touring among the villages with great earnestness, and with some measure of success.

During the summer of 1863, Mr. Douglass' health broke down, and he with his family went to Coromandel, by the sea, where they remained several months. Soon after his return to Nellore, he baptized four converts, to whom he thus refers: "As I stood in the water, and these trophies of a Saviour's love came down one after another into the water, my heart said, amen; the heathen shall yet come in crowds. Many Brahmans were spectators. The scene will not be forgotten on earth, and I trust will not be disowned in heaven."

In 1864, a new departure in the line of itinerating was made. Up to that time the native preachers had not engaged in this work, except as they accompanied the missionary. Now they were sent out alone. In September of that year, a number of them made a tour among the villages in the region of Ongole. They were gone about two months, and brought back a most encouraging report of the work in that neighborhood.

For want of money this work had to be suspended, and that too, at just the time when the missionary could join in it. This was a painful experience. With the language at his command, the people ready to hear, a few able and faithful helpers eager for the work, and the weather favorable for traveling, to be kept in the station for want of money was very trying, indeed. But there was no help for it, for mission work cannot be carried on without money.

The schools at this time were in a most hopeful condition. The annual examinations proved that good and faithful work had been done. And better still, the Spirit of God was among them, and four or five were hopefully converted. The baptizing of these converts closed Mr. Douglass' mission work, and he left for home in April, 1865.

CHAPTER V.

The question of abandoning the mission again presented. Mr. Clough joins Mr. Jewett. Encouragements in the work. A visit to Ongole. Conversion of Periah. His earnestness in the work of making Christ known. Mr. Jewett's appeal for two more men. The in-gathering at Tullakondapaud. Depletion at Nellore.

A T the annual meeting of the Missionary Union held in Providence, in 1862, the question "Shall the Telugu mission be abandoned?" came up for the third and last time. A resolution recommending its abandonment was offered, and its passage urgently demanded. It would no doubt have passed, but for the influence of the corresponding secretary, the Rev. Dr. Warren, who plead that the question might be deferred until the arrival of Mr. Jewett, who was then on his way home. This was reluctantly agreed to, and it was virtually the settlement of that oft-repeated question, for when Mr. Jewett arrived, he simply declined to entertain any proposition to abandon the mission. He had spent thirteen years among a people he had loved, had already gathered some precious fruit, and had strong faith that "the Lord had much people" among the Telugus. He told the Executive Committee, in the most emphatic terms, of his determination never to give up the Telugu Mission. If the Union declined to aid him, he would go back alone, and live and, if need be, die among the Telugus. Such courage, faith,

60

and determination were not to be resisted; hence it was resolved to return him, if health was restored, and a new man with him.

Mr. Jewett, accompanied by the Rev. John E. Clough and wife, sailed from Boston, November 30, 1864; reached Madras, March 26, and Nellore, April 22, 1865. Mrs. Jewett remained at home on account of her children until December 5, 1865, when she sailed from Boston and joined her husband April 26, 1866.

After getting settled in their new home, Mr. and Mrs. Clough commenced the study of Telugu, and early began to make use of the few words they had learned, in speaking to the people about the great salvation. Their zeal and success in Nellore were an indication of their greater work and more abundant success in the field God was preparing for them at Ongole.

Soon after the missionaries arrived in Nellore, an earnest spirit seemed to pervade the mission. The missionaries began to predict large ingatherings in the near future. On the first Sunday in November, Mr. Clough baptized four converts, which greatly encouraged both the missionaries and the little church which had struggled so long against adverse circumstances. One of these converts was a lad of much promise connected with the boarding school. The others were women with families, two of whom were notorious for their bad characters and opposition to Christianity.

The missionaries sent home an urgent appeal for two more men. One of these was to be stationed at Alloor, eighteen miles north of Nellore, and one at Ramapatam, forty-five miles north of Nellore. Although Mr. Clough

had been designated to Ongole, he expressed a readiness
to go to either of these new stations. But subsequent
events will show that God had arranged all that.

In March, 1866, Mr. and Mrs. Jewett, Mr. Clough and
Canakiah made a visit to Ongole, having special reference
to seeing Periah, who wanted to see the missionaries and
to be baptized. He was not in Ongole, as had been expected, but returned in a few days. So eager, indeed, was
he do this that he left a meal unfinished, at which he was
seated when the intelligence of the arrival of the missionaries came to him. In relating his experience, Periah said :
"Four years ago, I went north to Ellore, and there heard
for the first time the gospel from Mr. Alexander, of the
Church Mission. After that I went to Palacole, and
heard from Mr. Bowden, and saw the native Christians.
After my return, the Lord enlightened my mind, and I
began laboring for the conversion of my family. After
eighteen months, my wife was converted, and several
others were awakened."

This simple recitation of God's dealings with this man,
belonging to a class almost too degraded to be despised,
unable to read a word, and yet giving such a clear testimony, made a deep impression on the missionaries. The
simplicity of his story, the sincerity of his faith, and the
ardor of his love, all testified to the saving power of God's
grace.

His wife, in the same spirit of simplicity, faith, and love,
told the artless story of her conversion. "These," said
Mr. Jewett, "were some of the happiest moments of my
life. I was ready in a moment to baptize them." The
little company proceeded to a tank about two miles off,

History of the Telugu Mission.

and there as the sun was setting, the two happy converts were baptized. These were the first converts from the Madagas—the class from which the great mass of the Ongole Christians have come.

Periah made the most of his opportunity, while the missionaries were in Ongole, to get all the knowledge he could about the new religion, for he was anxious to become a witness for Christ. In course of time, he became an earnest minister of Jesus Christ, and is still the patriarch of the Ongole preachers.

Two months later, Canakiah, Rungiah, and Rungashia, three Nellore native preachers, went on a preaching tour to the northwest, to a territory including Periah's village. They were greatly astonished to find Periah burning with zeal for the souls of his fellow-men. It stirred them up greatly to find him far ahead of themselves in his desire to preach. He used to stir them up long before daybreak to go to villages at a distance. The weather was at its hottest, and Periah would carry a great pot of buttermilk on his head for the preachers to drink when thirsty. These labors were greatly blessed, and when the preachers returned to Nellore, they reported that probably two hundred people in the region around Tullakondapaud were believing in Christ. From that time on Mr. Clough became impatient till he was permitted to proceed to Ongole.

After returning from Ongole, Mr. Jewett baptized three converts in Nellore. One was the only surviving son of Christian Nursu, already spoken of. The second was a Tamil woman, formerly of Madras, who had been an immoral character; for several months, she had attended the chapel, and after a time manifested a deep abhorrence of her past life, frequently rose for prayers, and at last found peace in believing in Christ. The other convert was a pupil of the boarding school.

In concluding his annual report for 1866, Mr. Jewett expresses an earnest wish that the Board would keep in mind the appeal for two men, one for Alloor and one for Ramapatam. This he said would by no means supply the demands of so vast a field, but it would give a line of stations from Nellore to Ongole, and would be a good beginning toward what eventually must be done.

The year 1867 was one of great blessings. Mr. Clough had removed to Ongole the previous year, and the first in-gathering had taken place at Tullakondapaud. Refer-ring to that event, Mr. Jewett wrote: "I am glad Mr. Clough is in possession of ample means, and what is better still, that he has found a field ripe for the harvest. Are you not now glad that we tugged so hard to get a footing in Ongole? Has not God put honor on native agency?"

A severe blow fell on the mission at this time in the death of Venkataswamy, a valuable helper in Nellore. He was bookkeeper, Sunday-school teacher, and preacher all in one, and his loss seemed almost irreparable. He was taken ill with cholera January 13, and died the same night. He was one of the brightest trophies of redeeming grace that had yet been won in the Telugu Mission, and his end was peaceful and glorious beyond expression. But his departure for the better world left a sad vacancy in the mission.

This sad event, together with the withdrawal of laborers to the Ongole field, drove the little band at Nellore to make the most of what remained; and committing all to him who is able to make possible the greatest results from the smallest means, they labored on in faith. A special effort was made to arouse the church to the importance of every member doing his best to make Christ known all around. The result was the accession of ten precious converts.

CHAPTER VI.

BRANCHING OUT.

THE Rev. A. V. Timpany and wife joined the mission at Nellore in May, 1868. Here they remained studying the language and assisting Mr. Jewett till February, 1870, when they removed to Ramapatam. The Rev. Jno. McLaurin and wife arrived in Madras, February 11, 1870, and proceeded at once to Ramapatam. The Rev. E. Bullard also joined the mission that year, reaching Nellore in November. He was the first of our missionaries to come out *via* the Suez Canal. A fuller account of these brethren will be found in connection with the stations that formed the scene of their labors.

By the end of 1870, the number of church-members was one hundred and eighty-three, with fifty pupils in the training school. There were seven out-stations, with an aggregate attendance of one hundred. The government grant-in-aid to these schools was two hundred and eighty-eight rupees, showing a marked increase over all preceding years. It is due to Mrs. Jewett to say that much of this prosperity was owing to her indefatigable efforts, especially in connection with school work. It seemed, therefore, little other than an adverse providence, when in 1869 she was obliged to leave her husband and the work she loved so well, and return home in the interests of her children. Thanks to the Woman's Board, such painful experiences, if not entirely removed, are at least considerably modified by the excellent "Home" at Newton Centre.

After Mrs. Jewett's departure, Dr. Jewett labored on alone till April, 1874, when he left Nellore to find a much-needed rest at home.

The Rev. D. Downie and wife were designated to the Telugu mission, February 25, 1873, and arrived in Nellore, December 10th of that year. Mr. Downie relieved Dr. Jewett of his station, January 1, 1874, and of the mission treasury in March. It was no easy task for the young missionaries to take up the work of a veteran before they had been in the country two months. The policy of giving new missionaries at least the first year free from all responsibility, except that of studying the language, is a wise one which should be departed from only in very exceptional cases. To be thrust into the charge of a large station before a good start in the language has been made, is a wrong first to the man, second to the mission, and third to the Union. It is a wrong to the man, because the chances are either that he will attempt to do his work through an interpreter, a crutch which he will find difficult to lay aside while the pressure of work continues ; or he will acquire a slovenly style of speech, half English and half Telugu. It is a wrong to the mission, for other things being equal, a man is useful to the mission in proportion to his thorough knowledge of the language of the people. It is a wrong to the Union, because by assumption of burdens he is unable to carry, at the very outset of his career a missionary is very liable to injure his health and prematurely break down. The other extreme of doing absolutely nothing the first year or two but study, is by no means justified by what has just been said. Such cases are not altogether unknown, but fortunately they are rare. There is much a new man can do and ought to do the first year besides study, but it should be as an assistant without responsibility, and subordinate to his chief work of acquiring the language.

In October, 1874, a devastating flood, the greatest Nellore had ever known up to that time, visited the town, carrying ruin and desolation in its course. By the breaching of the Pennar river, which flows about half a mile north of the mission compound, the course of the river was changed, and for three days it rushed through the compound. The houses were built of mud, and crumbled down one after the other, leaving the sticks and straw floating around. As the huts in the neighboring hamlet were destroyed, many of the people, Christian and heathen, came to the missionaries for shelter, carrying all their earthly possessions on their heads. The men we admitted into the chapel, the women and children being cared for in the west end of the bungalow. For three days all waited the subsiding of the waters. The missionaries had no

History of the Telugu Mission.   NELLORE SCHOOL-GIRLS.

stores of supplies, and only one chicken on hand. The third day of the flood the only loaf of bread in town was brought to them by the kind-hearted baker, who, though a heathen outwardly, had for years given evidence of being a Christian at heart. For a while after the flood, little could be done but remove debris and rebuild. In the compound, only the bungalow, chapel, and girls' school-house remained standing, the last two in a damaged condition, necessitating speedy removal. These were dark days.

In response to an appeal for a new girls' school, the Woman's Board of Boston sent two thousand three hundred dollars. With this and a government grant-in-aid of three thousand rupees, the present schoolhouse and dormitories were erected in 1876. The opening services were attended by nearly all the European and Eurasian people of Nellore, together with our own native Christians. The collector of the district presided and delivered a most kind and encouraging address. One of the girls read a portion of Scripture in Telugu, and the singing by the school gave much pleasure and satisfaction to all. The building was pronounced by government to be " a most suitable and substantial building."

With the enlarged and improved accommodations, the number of girls was greatly increased. There were thirty girls in the boarding school, and a considerable number of day scholars. Two years before it was with difficulty that even Christian parents could be induced to send their children to school ; now many applications for admission had to be refused. There was also at this time a great demand for village schools ; but suitable Christian teachers were hard to find, and there was no money to spend on village schools taught by heathen teachers. Where suitable teachers could be found schools were maintained.

The year 1877 is memorable as the year when the great famine began. As the famine extended over the larger part of the mission territory, and engaged so large a portion of the missionaries' time in nearly all the stations, and was in fact the most important item of the mission's history during two years, it will be treated in a separate chapter.

When the writer first came to Nellore, Dr. Jewett called his attention to three young men of the Reddi, or farmer caste, living at Razupalem, one of the out-stations of Nellore, who, he said, if not already Christians, he believed would some day come to Christ: and then he added, his eyes gleaming with delight at the thought, " When we get the Reddis, brother Downie, our mission will be made." Four years after the conversation, the youngest of the brothers was baptized. He is a strong-built man over six feet in height, and with a passion for knowledge not often seen. It was a struggle for him to throw off the shackles of caste, and leave his family. For three days, his people hung around trying to persuade him to return : " Just for one day to comfort his weeping family," s) they said. But their intention was to burn with red-hot gold the tongue that had confessed Christ. Ramiah, that is the young man's name, took his place in school, sitting on the same bench with boys scarcely reaching his waist, and began his studies. In due time he passed from the station school to the seminary. When he graduated, the question where he should labor came up. The missionary had a firm conviction that Ramiah's field of labor should be his own village, and among his own people. Then ensued a struggle which neither the missionary nor Ramiah is likely to forget. To live in the mission compound surrounded by Christian friends, was one thing; but to go and live in his own village, and among his own people, who now regarded him as an out-caste or Pariah, was a very different thing. After a good deal of discussion, he finally consented to go. He was gone about ten days, but returned, and said he could not stand it. His friends abused him and entreated him: "Is it not," they said, "enough that you should disgrace us by leaving your caste, without coming here to remind us daily of our disgrace? Go, live where you like, but let us not be put to shame by your presence among us." It did seem like a hard case, and for a time the missionary was half inclined to yield; but he well knew that if he did, Ramiah's influence among the caste people would be forever gone. He prayed over it, and got Ramiah to pray over it; reasoned, counselled, and encouraged, and finally said: "Ramiah, you must go to Razupalem, and live. You may save your people. God seems to me to call you there, and there you must go." Ramiah said he could not, and would not. Again he was urged to pray over it. Two days later he came with a smiling, but determined face, and said, "I'll go to Razupalem and live or die, as the case may be." He went, and when his people saw his determination to live among them, and labor for their spiritual good, all opposition immediately disappeared, and so far from abusing him, they have ever since treated him and his family with kindness.

Ramiah has gathered around him.a flourishing little congregation, and though none of the caste people have as yet believed, they listen respectfully to the word preached, and there is every reason to hope that they will yet turn to Christ in large numbers.

For forty years the thatch-covered zayat built by Mr. Day had done good service as the "Lone Star" place of worship. But it had long ceased to be suitable or worthy of the mission. About the close of 1879, Mr. Clough, while on a visit to Nellore, said to the missionary : "If you build a chapel that will accommodate five hundred people, I will give toward it a hundred rupees." This was precisely what the missionary wanted. A subscription book was opened, headed by a liberal subscription from J. Grose, Esq., collector of the district. A number of the missionaries followed with one hundred rupees each. The native Christians of Nellore gave to the full extent of their ability. In this way enough was raised to lay the foundations.

On the 29th of December, 1879, the corner-stone was laid with appropriate ceremonies. The stone had been dug from the ruins of a Hindu temple, and in the receptacle, which once contained the emblems of idolatry, were placed a copy of the Telugu Bible, the "Telugu Baptist," and copies of our American denominational papers. Dr. Jewett, Messrs. Clough, Williams, and others were present. The ceremony of laying the stone was performed by J. Grose, Esq., collector of the district. Here the work stopped for want of funds for nearly a year, when enough was in hand to raise the walls. Again the work had to stop. The time was approaching when the missionary

THE NELLORE CHAPEL.

would have to go home, but he could not bear the thought of leaving the chapel in its unfinished state. Some advised him to borrow the money, and trust to getting it at home, but that he did not like to do. The matter was laid before the Lord, and in due time an appropriation of one thousand five hundred dollars came from the Executive Committee, and thus the chapel was completed, and dedicated the Sunday before the missionary left Nellore. The cost of the chapel was nine thousand four hundred and sixty-eight rupees.

One of the most remarkable events of this period was the visit of the Rev. S. F. Smith, D. D., and wife. The profound interest Dr. Smith has had in the mission almost from its origin made this visit one of peculiar interest and pleasure. Dr. Smith has published his experiences in the Telugu Mission in his " Rambles in Mission Fields," and to that very excellent little volume we refer our readers for a racy and most interesting account of his impressions of the work at Nellore and elsewhere.

The Rev. J. F. Burditt was transferred from Ongole to Nellore in April, 1882, to relieve Mr. Downie who, with his family, sailed from Madras on the 16th of the same month for the United States. Mr. Burditt carried on the work till Mr. Downie's return, October 13, 1884, when he removed to Udayagiri.

While at home, Mr. Downie received from Mr. William Bucknell, of Philadelphia, three thousand five hundred dollars for the erection of a girls' seminary in Nellore. This building was completed in 1886. The school has a threefold object. 1. A Bible school for the training of Bible women. 2. A normal school for the training of teachers.

3. An industrial school for instruction in useful occupations. The school has no appropriations from the Society. The students earn their own board and clothes. The aim is not only to make the school entirely self-supporting, but also to aid in supporting the other station schools.

Miss Jennie E. Wayte arrived in Nellore, October 13, 1884, in company with Mr. and Mrs. Downie. She was designated by the Woman's Board of Boston to Bible and Zenana work in Nellore. She also has charge of the girls' and boys' schools, and indeed she, like every other good missionary, is ready to do cheerfully and with her might what her hands find to do.

The Rev. J. Heinrichs arrived in Madras, November 1, 1889, designated to Vinukonda. But in anticipation of Mrs. Downie's return home, the Executive Committee authorized Mr. and Mrs. Heinrichs to proceed to Nellore, and there spend the first year in the study of Telugu. This gave Mr. Heinrichs exceptionally good advantages in acquiring the language, and at the same time enabled him to render valuable assistance in the work at Nellore.

Dr. Ashmore, then Home Secretary of the Missionary Union, paid a visit to the mission in the early part of 1890. He arrived first in Madras and then proceeded to Secunderabad, thence through Guntur to Bapatla and Ongole. Here a special meeting of the missionaries was called to meet him. From January 9th to 14th a delightful time was spent in consultation respecting the needs of the mission, and in prayer and conference. On Sunday, Dr. Ashmore preached through an interpreter to a large congregation of native people, and in the evening to a goodly company in English. It was arranged that

History of the Telugu Mission.
GIRLS' SCHOOL AND BOYS' SCHOOL, BUCKNELL MEMORIAL, NELLORE.

Dr. Ashmore should accompany Dr. Clough on an evangelistic tour over a portion of the Ongole field, where Dr. Clough believed many converts were awaiting the ordinance of baptism. But before this could be carried out, Dr. Clough's health was such that the plan was abandoned.

From Ongole our visitor went to Ramapatam, visited the seminary, addressed the students, and then came to Nellore. His three days at Nellore will be remembered for many a year. He addressed both the English and Telugu Sunday-schools, and preached to the Telugu church in the morning and the English church in the evening. Both congregations were large, and listened with rapt attention. The native Christians tendered Dr. Ashmore a reception at the bungalow. In their address of welcome they had but one request—two more missionaries for Nellore.

This visit of Dr. Ashmore was an inspiration and a benediction both to the missionaries and the native Christians.

For more than a year the state of Mrs. Downie's health was far from satisfactory, and at times gave rise to considerable anxiety and even alarm. Her daughter, Alice, also had reached that age when both health and education would seriously suffer by a further stay in India, and hence it was decided best that they should return home. They sailed from Madras, March 16, 1890. Mr. Downie accompanied them as far as Colombo, and then returned to his lonely quarters to continue his work for two years longer, when he hoped to be permitted to rejoin his family.

In just one year and one month from the time of Dr. Ashmore's visit, we were again permitted to welcome to Nellore his successor as Home Secretary, the Rev. H. C. Mabie, D. D., an l his friend, the Rev. Dr. Waterman. By the arrival of an urgent cable message from the Executive Committee to return home at once, Dr. Mabie was about to cut short his visit to the Telugu Mission, and hence called a conference of the brethren to meet him in Nellore, which would be the only station he could visit. This cable message was sent to Nellore while Dr. Murdock was ill. Some days later, Dr. Murdock became aware of what had been done, and immediately sent another message : " Mabie finish Telugu Mission." This message reached Nellore while Dr. Mabie was addressing the people in the Nellore chapel. There was a very deep conviction that this was a direct answer to the earnest prayers that had gone up to God, that he would guide all our plans and deliberations. This changed Dr. Mabie's plans, and enabled him to proceed to Ramapatam, Ongole, and Cumbum. These were happy, blessed days in Nellore, and Dr. Mabie left a profound impression on the missionaries and native Christians, that will keep for him a warm place in their hearts.

At Ramapatam, Dr. Mabie addressed the students of the Seminary, and then visited each of the classes separately, observing the methods of instruction and imparting words of counsel and cheer. The closing chapter on Ongole will tell more of this visit

NELLORE SCHOOL BOYS.

CHAPTER VII.

ONGOLE.

ONGOLE is situated on the Great Northern Trunk Road, one hundred and eighty-two miles north of Madras, and ten miles from the Bay of Bengal. It is the second largest town in the Nellore District, and is the headquarters of the sub-collector. Its population in 1891 was nine thousand two hundred.

The Rev. John Everett Clough and Ongole are names that can never be dissociated : the one naturally suggests the other. As we trace the history of the mission at Ongole we shall find unmistakable evidence of God's wonder-working power in the great work that has been accomplished. We have seen how God had already begun to bless a feeble native agency in the awakening and conversion of souls on that great field before the missionary arrived there, and we shall see how he continued it when the work passed into new and inexperienced hands. And

77

yet, while we recognize the work as God's work, we cannot fail to see that he raised up and especially fitted Mr. Clough as the agent through whom he was to accomplish it. . If we were called upon to name Mr. Clough's special qualifications for the particular work to which he has been called, we should say that they were these : A capacity to command the situation and to marshal its resources; a sound constitution and an indomitable spirit; a strong love for Christ and the souls of men; a successful term of pioneer service in the Western States, and a strong faith both in God and in himself as God's appointed agent for the accomplishment of a great work.

We have already noted Mr. and Mrs. Clough's arrival in Nellore in 1865, and the enthusiastic manner in which they entered upon their work. It was evident from the very beginning that they had come to India for a purpose, and they burned to have it accomplished. That purpose was to preach Christ to the Telugus. Hence it was that before Mr. Clough could speak half a dozen sentences in Telugu correctly, he began talking to the people in the streets and bazaars of Nellore.

On the evening of September 12th, 1866, Mr. and Mrs. Clough and their little boy Allen left Nellore for Ongole. After a somewhat tiresome journey, the party reached Ongole on the morning of the 17th.

One of the first things a missionary wants in a new station, after a place to cover his own head, is a chapel. Mr. Clough had scarcely settled in Ongole before he set to work to get a building that should be chapel and schoolhouse combined. The estimated cost of such a building as he proposed to erect was one thousand five hundred rupees; but the actual cost was two thousand three hundred and forty rupees, of which the sum of two thousand and ninety rupees was raised by subscriptions in India, and the balance was charged to mission funds.

But Mr. Clough did not wait for the completion of his chapel before he began preaching and gathering in converts. He immediately arranged the forces at his command, and set them to work. From Nellore he brought three able assistants. Two were preachers, and one was a colporteur. The preachers preached in the streets of Ongole and surrounding villages, and the colporteur accompanied them or followed them, selling his tracts and portions of the Bible. Mrs. Clough opened a school, and soon had ten pupils, while Mr. Clough supervised the whole, and usually spent the evenings in preaching in and about Ongole.

Tullakondapaud is a village which deserves especial mention as the place where occurred the first revival, or spiritual ingathering, on the Ongole field. It is also the village of Periah, the first convert from the Madigas, the class from which nearly all the Ongole Christians have come, who was baptized by Mr. Jewett, when he was at Ongole in 1866. Tullakondapaud is about forty miles west of Ongole. Ever since Periah's conversion and baptism, the preachers and colporteurs had been making occasional visits to this village, spending several days at a time in company with Periah, preaching and praying and talking with the people. Periah had also made several visits to Ongole to see the missionary, taking with him all who were anxious to know about the new religion. From

these visits, as well as from the reports brought by the
preachers, it was evident that a spirit of inquiry prevailed
in that region.   As soon, therefore, as the week of prayer
was closed, Mr. Clough determined to make a visit to
Tullakondapaud and the regions beyond.   He intended
to spend several weeks on this tour, but a little experience
soon taught him that he was not prepared for it.   The
roads were rough, and he traveled in a bullock cart by
night, halting by day to rest the bullocks.   He made
slow progress, of course, but it gave him an opportunity
to preach in such villages as were near enough to the
road to be reached on foot.

At Tullakondapaud, he pitched his tent in a tamarind
grove, and sent word to all the surrounding villages that
he had come to visit them, and asked them to come to the
tent and see him.   The following day, some thirty or forty
people arrived, bringing with them a supply of food to
last several days, and also a change of clothing to put on
after they were baptized; they said they had come to
learn more about Jesus, but that they believed already,
and wanted to be baptized.

For five days the meetings were held.   At the end of
the fifth day, January 20, twenty-eight converts were
baptized on profession of their faith in Christ.   It was a
precious season which Mr. Clough will probably never
forget.   Moved by some such impulse as moved Peter to
say on the Mount of Transfiguration, "Let us make here
three tabernacles," Mr. Clough expressed the wish that
he might spend at least six months of the year in tents,
moving about the country preaching Christ.   But to do
that he must be better equipped; and besides Ongole as

the centre of operations had claims which could not be neglected. This latter consideration led Mr. Clough to renew the appeal for two more men, and predicted that the time was near when the Telugus would come to Christ by thousands.

This precious work of grace, while it was an inspiration to the missionaries, and doubtless caused joy in heaven, had a very different effect upon the surrounding heathen. Satan does not willingly relinquish his hold on men. No sooner had these converts abandoned his service and entered the service of the Lord, than the devil put it into the hearts of his emissaries to persecute the poor Christians. Water from the public wells was denied them, and false charges of crime were trumped up against them, and they were thrust into prison. But the Lord delivered them, and the false accusers were publicly reprimanded and cautioned to let the Christians alone. This deliverance, and the addition of others from the same region rejoiced the missionaries greatly.

It has been a wonder to many why it is that the Christians have come almost exclusively from the lower classes. It need not have been so. Had the missionaries been disposed to pander to the caste prejudices of the Hindus as the Roman Catholics, and even some Protestants do, and excluded the poor out-castes, or at all events given them a separate and lower place in the church, many caste people would no doubt have professed Christianity. But they could not do that without violating their consciences. What a struggle it cost to take and maintain this position may be illustrated by the following incident, which took place at Ongole. In January, 1867, a number of caste

F

people came to Ongole, and professed faith in Christianity and asked to be baptized. But they had heard of the
Madigas, who had been baptized at Tullakondapaud, and
objected to being in the same church with them. The
missionary said they were forty miles away, and could
not harm them. For a while this seemed to pacify them.
But in April, twelve more converts came from Tullakondapaud to be baptized. The missionary almost hoped
they would fail in the examination. But they gave good
evidence of conversion. Here was a dilemma. Could
these converts be rejected to please a heathen prejudice?
The missionaries sought counsel of God. Without design
on his part, Mr. Clough turned to 1 Cor. 1 : 26–29 : "For
ye see your calling, brethren, how that not many wise
men after the flesh, not many mighty, not many noble,
are called : but God hath chosen the foolish things of the
world to confound the wise; and God hath chosen the
weak things of the world to confound the things which are
mighty ; and base things of the world, and things which are
despised, hath God chosen, yea, and things which are not,
to bring to nought things which are : that no flesh should
glory in his presence." In a separate room, at the same
time, Mrs. Clough read this same passage, yet with no
knowledge of what her husband was doing. Coming from
their closets each related what had transpired. They had
no longer any doubt as to God's will. The converts
were baptized, much to the disgust of the caste people,
who said : "If these are received, we cannot enter your
church."

This event, though apparently unpropitious, was probably one of the most fortunate circumstances in the history

of the mission. Had the missionaries yielded to their
own inclinations, and admitted the caste people in preference to the low out-castes, the doors of the church would
have been effectually closed and barred against all non-
caste converts; the mission would have become a caste
mission—a semi-Christian mission, more like the Brahmo
Somaj than a Christian church. It would have taken a
higher social standing: more of the well-to-do classes would
have joined it, and it would have exerted a wider influence
among the educated and wealthy. But on the other hand,
instead of fourteen stations, there would have been perhaps three or four; instead of forty thousand members, a
few hundred would probably be all that could be numbered.

But infinitely more important than the question of
numbers, rank or wealth is that of character   It is by no
means either said or implied that a Christian from the
out-castes is better than one from the caste people. On
the contrary, other things being equal, the caste convert is
to be preferred. A few of the low caste converts with
even a limited education have shown powers of mind
equal if not superior to the average Brahman; but this is
by no means common. It will take many generations of
Christian training and education before the Christians
from the Pariah class can be raised to the intellectual
level of the Brahman, and other caste people. If, therefore, the caste people were really and truly converted
there can be no doubt that it would hasten the day when
the church will be able to stand alone. Indeed, it is the
faith of many that till that day comes, that is, till the
caste people are reached and brought in, the church will
not attain an independent standing in India. But it is in-

finitely better that the coming in of the caste people should be delayed than that they should bring into the church a religious caste. Hence the wisdom of God in calling the poor out-castes first. When the caste people come—as come they must—it will only be when their caste has been thoroughly broken and abandoned. This will be the strongest possible evidence of the genuineness of their conversion.

By the close of 1867, the Ongole Church had increased from eight members at its organization to seventy-five; the new chapel was completed and paid for, almost wholly from funds collected in the country. The gospel had been preached to the people of over eight hundred villages, and over seventy thousand pages of tracts and Scripture portions had been distributed. Besides these labors of the missionary and his assistants, Mrs. Clough had conducted a school in Ongole, and frequently went out with the wives of the preachers to labor among the village women. Thus the good seed of the kingdom was sown broadcast, and even while sowing the seed, the Lord of the harvest graciously permitted the sowers to gather in many sheaves of precious grain. But what appeared to be a shower of divine grace, was simply a few drops before a more copious rain.

In his report of 1867, Mr. Clough referred to an Anglo-vernacular school he had started, from which he had hoped for good results. But soon after, he changed his mind and wrote to the Board that he had closed the school, dismissed his English teacher, and determined, by God's help, to be "a missionary of one idea," and devote all his energies to raising up a class of native helpers to preach Christ to the Telugus in their own tongue. The Corresponding Secretary strongly commended this course, and, quoting Mr. Clough's words, said : " They are very suggestive, and may well be pondered by all."

. Perhaps no one pondered these words more than Mr. Clough himself, and with the result that he long ago ceased to be the " missionary of one idea " that he thought he was. As far back as 1875 he started the movement which resulted in the present high school, which is precisely what he discarded in 1867. Circumstances alter cases, and the missionary who can recognize the changed condition of the people and change his policy accordingly, is wiser than he who persists on a given course irrespective of the new conditions. Mr. Clough was probably right in discarding Anglo-vernacular schools in 1867, but not more so than in advocating them in 1875. They were not needed then ; now they are.

CHAPTER VIII.

IN the garden of the Ongole compound Mr. Clough constructed a baptistery, which was dedicated on the first of August, 1869, by the baptism of forty-two converts. It was a most interesting occasion, and filled the missionaries with great joy and thanksgiving. To some extent they had in this baptismal scene a glimpse of the greater similar events before them. But they little dreamed that in less than ten years from that day more than ten thousand would be added to their number by baptism.

An hour after these first baptisms in the Ongole baptistery the company gathered in the chapel and celebrated the Lord's Supper. The Christians were not disposed to return to their villages, but lingered on to hear more, and to rehearse their troubles occasioned by the heathen. Until nearly midnight the missionary continued, advising, exhorting, and encouraging them.

Soon after this, Mr. Clough made a tour to the west as far as Cumbum. The whole tour from beginning to end

86

History of the Telugu Mission.   Page 77.

REV. JOHN E. CLOUGH.

furnished unmistakable evidences that the good seed had been scattered, and in many places was taking root. Near Cumbum, some fifty or sixty asked to be baptized. Of these, twenty-five were received and baptized in the Goondlacumma river. This was the beginning of the Cumbum field, which now bids fair to rival even Ongole in fruitfulness.

At Markapur, another important town about twenty miles north of Cumbum, Mr. Clough found a few Christians who had been sorely persecuted by their heathen neighbors. Some of them had been cast into prison. Some of them were too weak to withstand the persecution and went back into heathenism; but most of them stood firm, and through the missionary's influence were soon delivered from their persecutors. This, of course, gave courage to the faltering, and no doubt influenced others to join the Christians.

In November, seventy-four were baptized in Ongole. This was the largest number that had yet been received at one time. Mrs. Clough, in writing about it, said that although they had expected great things from the Lord, this was beyond their expectations, and a rebuke to their little faith. In December, Mr. Clough made another tour to the district of Cumbum. Great crowds everywhere gathered to hear the word preached, and as the result of the effort three hundred and twenty-four were baptized. Thus the year 1869 closed with a total increase of six hundred and forty-eight.

In 1870, the work was continued with unabated zeal and success. Another trip was made to Cumbum, the Rev. Jno. McLaurin being of the company. This was a fortunate circumstance, for on the way Mr. Clough was taken seriously ill, and although this cut short the tour, a large number of converts was baptized by Mr. McLaurin. Mr. Clough went to Ramapatam to rest awhile by the sea, hoping thus to be able to continue his work. He derived benefit from this, and so was able to remain in India through the year.

During 1871, Mr. Clough made three extensive tours over his field accompanied by Mr. McLaurin. As the latter was to succeed Mr. Clough in Ongole, this introduction to the work was of great value. By the end of this year the Ongole Church numbered one thousand six hundred and fifty-eight. In November, Mr. McLaurin removed his family from Ramapatam to Ongole, and in February, 1872, after seven years of incessant labor, Mr. Clough and his family returned to the United States for needed rest and recuperation.

Mr. and Mrs. McLaurin had by this time been in the country two years, having landed in Madras, February 11, 1870. They went direct to Ramapatam, where they at once began the study of Telugu. Mr. McLaurin had a passion for language, and speedily acquired an exceptionally good command of the Telugu. This, with his opportunities of mingling with the people while touring with Mr. Clough, and thus practicing what he had learned, fitted him in an eminent degree for the great work which lay before him. Few missionaries are so early called upon to assume charge of a field involving graver responsibilities, harder work, or the exercise of greater discretion; and fewer still could have discharged the responsible duties more successfully.

VILLAGE PREACHING.

Still, the Christians did not like the prospect of parting with the only missionary they had known, and exchanging him for one whom they did not know. This spirit of dissatisfaction was manifest even before Mr. Clough left Ongole, and no sooner had he gone than it broke out into open rebellion. But Mr. McLaurin's discretion, firmness, patience, and kindness soon convinced the people that he was their friend, and would do for them all that they could reasonably expect him or any other to do. In addition to this trouble in Ongole, a panic had seized the Christians at Cumbum, owing to a violent type of fever having broken out. The heathen declared that the Christians were the cause of it. The gods were angry because they had forsaken their worship, and this fever was sent as a punishment. As the custom is, a great sacrifice had to be made to appease the anger of the gods, and the Christians were told that they must join in it. Some did so, while others stood firm in their refusal. A number of boys from this part of the field were at school in Ongole. To them Mr. McLaurin gave medicine and such instruction as he could, and sent them off to Cumbum to care for their sick relatives and friends. This accomplished a double purpose. It reduced the number of discontented ones in Ongole, and diverted the minds of some of them from making mischief to doing good; and it also reassured many at Cumbum who were wavering in their faith. Before the year closed all these troubles were ended, and the people rallied around Mr. McLaurin just as they had done around Mr. Clough.

During the first year Mr. McLaurin travelled over a very large portion of the field, preaching in a large number of villages, including Vinukonda and Nursaraopett, now flourishing stations. There had been seventeen preachers and three colporteurs employed. The latter had sold six thousand five hundred tracts and eight hundred Bible portions, besides giving many away. There were one hundred and thirteen pupils in the compound school, ten of whom entered the seminary that year. There were also twenty-two village schools.

The second year of Mr. McLaurin's labors in Ongole differed from the first only in degree. More traveling done, more converts baptized, and more instruction given. The Christians grew in grace and were gradually getting a better understanding of the principles of the gospel. During these two years Mr. McLaurin baptized one thousand one hundred and eighty-five, four hundred and seventy-seven the first year, and seven hundred and eight the second, which was the largest number thus far baptized in any one year. Mr. McLaurin handed over his charge to Mr. Clough, February 2, 1874, and immediately proceeded to Cocanada to organize the new Telugu mission of the Canadian Baptists.

Before setting out for America, Mr. Clough was commissioned to secure four new men for the mission and an endowment of fifty thousand dollars for the theological seminary. When this request was laid before the Executive Committee, it was thought to be a pretty large demand and much doubt was entertained as to the possibility of securing it. However, after a time consent was given to make the attempt, provided it could be done without interfering with the general collections of the Union. When this consent was secured, Mr. Clough set to work.

He issued circulars, and wrote letters, setting forth the claims and needs of the mission ; he traveled extensively, making his appeals to State Conventions, Associations, churches, and individuals.

The four men were appointed, and the fifty thousand dollars was secured. In achieving these results, Mr. Clough traveled twenty-nine thousand two hundred and sixteen miles, visited seventy cities, ninety-six churches, and delivered one hundred and sixty-two public addresses.

As soon as Mr. Clough returned from America, he resumed his work as in former years, until 1876, when the famine compelled him to turn his attention to saving the bodies as well as the souls of men.

CHAPTER IX.

THE GREAT FAMINE OF 1876–78.

The great famine. Famines common in India. Due to failure of the monsoons. Periodic in their visitations. Historic famines. Famine of 1876–78.
Failure of the monsoons. Apprehensions of famine. Prices of grain
increase. Grain riots. Importation of rice. Widespread distress. Deaths
from starvation. Horrors of the famine. Relief organized. Hindus first to
the rescue. Natives not always fairly represented. Charitable in disposition.
Many dependent ones. First indications of famine. Rumors of plenty.
Lack of measures to meet the emergency. Private charity abundant.
Thousands thus fed. Government action taken in Madras. Conspicuous
helpers. Work of the police. Relief elsewhere. Government works
established. Efficiency of government recognized. Appeals of missionaries for help. Relief in the Nellore compound. Mr. Clough as a contractor. The Mansion House fund. Formation of relief committees. The
Nellore Committee. Systematic visitation. Ruin to the small farmers.
Loss of cattle. Distress among other classes. Efforts to relieve it. Day
nurseries. Successful work by the Nellore Mission. Efficiency of the missionaries. Large loss of life despite relief measures. The natives not
ungrateful. Grateful thanks expressed.

ALTHOUGH the famine was common to the whole
mission, yet as the next chapter on the "Great
Ingathering" is so closely connected with the famine, it
seems very desirable that an account of it should be
given.

India has been subject to famines from the earliest historic periods. Large portions of the country always will
be liable to serious agricultural vicissitudes owing to
the uncertainty of the rainfall during the southwest and
northeast monsoons. The failure of these monsoon rains
has been the chief and almost exclusive cause of famines
in India. In a few instances, war has augmented and

92

even caused famine, but in the great majority of cases want of rain has been the sole cause. Thus of the forty-three famines of which we have records, all but three or four of them were caused by the failure of the monsoon rains. Except in Burma and East Bengal, where the rain never fails, and in Scinde, where it seldom or never comes and the people depend solely on river irrigation, some part of India suffers two years in every nine from famine. That is, taking the whole of India, a famine of some sort may be expected in one province or another every fourth or fifth year, and a bad famine every twelfth year. Or to put it in another form, the entire population of two hundred and fifty millions of people suffers from famine every half century.

The earliest famine of which we have any record was that of A. D. 1345, which was one of the very few that was caused more by the disturbed state of the country than by drought. It is said to have been very dreadful in its effects, especially around Delhi. The one of longest duration was that of A. D. 1396, which extended over the whole of South India, and decimated the entire country affected. It lasted for twelve years and in some sections there was a scarcity for thirty years. Of the famines of the present century, that of 1868–69, extended over the largest area, affecting two hundred and ninety-six thousand square miles, while the famine of 1876–78 affected the largest number of people, *viz.*, fifty-eight millions. It is of this last that we have now particularly to speak.

No one who was in South India toward the end of 1876 is likely to forget the intense anxiety with which the coming of the northeast monsoon was watched and prayed for. A cloud, though no bigger than a man's hand, was eagerly hailed as the possible harbinger of the long looked-for rain; but each cloud came and went, and still the heavens were as clear and bright as ever. Never perhaps were clear skies so thoroughly unappreciated.

As early as August a good deal of anxiety had begun to be felt, for the southwest monsoon failed to bring the usual amount of rain, and in some sections it was almost a total failure. In September, reports began to reach the newspapers regarding distress in some districts. Toward the end of October, no signs of the northeast monsoon being apparent, and the effect of the partial failure of the southwest monsoon being experienced in increasing measure in the central districts, it was apprehended that a dreadful famine was at hand; panic seized the people, and the grain merchants began to hoard up their grain and to import large quantities from other provinces. Prices rose to double and even treble the ordinary rates, and threats were made of " looting " grain bazaars. In some sections grain riots actually did take place, and although they were speedily checked yet they added much to the general anxiety of the government and panic of the people.

At this point the government of Madras thought it expedient to import grain, but the general government deprecated this as an infringement of the rights of private trade. If grain was imported at all it was to be strictly as a " reserve." Notwithstanding this, however, the Madras Government imported thirty thousand tons of rice and distributed it all over the affected districts, selling it at rates within the reach of the people.

The worst fears respecting the failure of the northeast monsoon were now fully realized, and the dreaded famine with all its untold horrors of pestilence, starvation, and death followed.

It would be difficult indeed to give in a few pages anything like an adequate description of the scenes that were daily brought to view during that dreadful time. Before relief operations were organized, our compounds were thronged by crowds of wretched, starving creatures begging for a morsel of food. Some of these were women with scarcely a rag of clothing to cover their bodies, and some of them with very little to cover, except skin and bones. Some were mothers of little babies vainly striving to extract a few drops of nourishment from their mother's empty breasts. The shrill cry of those babes, and the feeble wails of those mothers for food, were pitiful to hear. In the streets, even in towns like Nellore, it was no uncommon thing to see persons lying dead or dying from starvation or disease. The Rev. J. Herrick said: "On a recent tour I heard directly of the death of thirty persons from starvation. In one inclosure I saw a man lying on his back insensible. A little distance from him lay his wife in a half-conscious state with an infant trying to extract nourishment from her breast, and an older child lying in the same condition as its mother. The man died soon after. In another village of four families of twenty persons, nine died of starvation." Mr. Yorke of Dindigal said: "One of my schoolboys reported to me having seen thirty bodies brought down the river. In a small hamlet I was pained to see the children in a starving condition, yet none of them were beggars. A boy came with a bunch of greens to be cooked for the family; he exclaimed, "My eyes are dim," and falling to the ground, he died. Half the horrors of the famine have not and cannot be told."

F. Rowlandson, Esq., said : "At one place the faces of some of the children haunted us so much that we gave orders for two hundred of the worst cases to be collected. You should have seen them, for I could not hope to give you an adequate idea of their misery. In some, the last forces of their system seemed to have been expended in growing, and I never saw out of Doré's drawings, human beings whose length was so hideously disproportionate to their breadth. Others were tiny and wizened in every way, as if an attempt had been made to see into how small a compass a suffering body could be compressed. The whole party, after we had inspected them, were marched off to a relief camp, but over a hundred of them slipped away, and only ninety-six of them reached the new home. The poor wee runaways preferred, I suppose, the evils they knew of, bad as they were, to the horrid, vague unknown. Those that allowed themselves to be taken care of were fed, and soon that line of beauty, the curve, was substituted for the hideous famine angles." These are but isolated specimens of what might have been seen all over the country from the latter part of 1876 to the close of 1877.

It will be a surprise to some who read these pages to know that the first to enter the lists as dispensers of relief in this dire calamity were the Hindus themselves. Missionaries and others have not always been quite fair to the Hindus in this, as indeed in a good many other respects. Private charity in time of distress is a duty incumbent on every one who has the means wherewith to help his brother, and there are no people on the face of the earth more given to charity than the Hindus. The motive which prompts a Hindu to charity may be very different from that which prompts a Christian, and yet even here the difference, in many instances, may not be so great as at first appears. But we are not now speaking of motives, but of acts. In all Christian countries the poor are supported by the State, while in India they are supported by private charity. That is, beneficence to the poor in India is bestowed voluntarily, while in Christian countries it is rendered by government. Christianity in the concrete will not allow people to starve, but individual Christians do not feel so strongly as Hindus the claims of their religion in respect to charity. In Christian countries multitudes of beggars are supported by the State, who might and ought to be supported by their own relatives and friends. But on the other hand, it is a question whether this private charity does not foster pauperism. Certain it is, a fearfully large number of the population of India is wholly or in part dependent on the charity of their families and co-religionists. This is one of the many causes which keeps the great mass of the people so miserably poor, and which makes a famine a thing to be dreaded.

Among the first indications of the famine was the flocking of great crowds of men, women, and children to the cities and larger towns. In Madras especially this was most noticeable. In many of the rural districts a report had gotten abroad that in Madras "there were mountains of rice and oceans of ghee," and all they had to do was to go there and be fed. In this connection, Mr. Digby says : " The general public of Madras, as well as the government, was taken aback by the rapid manifestation of distress in October–December, 1876, and no organized measures were taken of a nature adequate to meet the need. The Friend-in-Need Society, a charitable institution for the relief of poor Europeans and Eurasians, strengthened its organization, but this was all. For the natives nothing was done on a scale commensurate with what was wanted. A suggestion was made that in Madras subscriptions should be raised, and non-official aid secured in relief measures, but the idea was looked upon coldly, or actively opposed, as in one of the daily journals of the city, where it was pointed out that the disaster was so terrible that only a great organization like that possessed by government could hope to cope with the difficulty. Consequently, nothing was done in an organized manner. Nevertheless, much charity was being displayed, particularly among the natives. There was scarcely a family which had not some poor relatives from the country who looked to them for food, which was cheerfully given ; not for a few weeks or months only, but in many cases for more than a year. Conversation with native gentlemen on this point has served to bring out many cases of heroic self-sacrifice. Half rations were cheerfully accepted by respectable people, so that their relatives might share with them such food as they had. Even, however, when all the wanderers who had kinsfolk in town were provided for, there were still many people who had no food, and in accordance with religious teaching, and the promptings of their own hearts, several Hindu gentlemen in the northern division of Madras fed daily a large number of people. Two members of the Chetty caste fed two thousand each ; one Modiliyar, two thousand ; two Chetties, two thousand, and one thousand five hundred respectively, and others smaller numbers, making altogether eleven thousand four hundred. The food supplied has been described as of a very poor character, being thin gruel, or congee of rice or raghi poured into their hands. In addition to these, hundreds of poor people congregated on the beach, were laying up for themselves a day of cruel reckoning, by living on the grains of rice sifted from the sea-sand. Early in December, the government felt it was bound to grapple with the distress manifested in the chief city of the presidency, and issued an order to the Commissioner of Police directing him to open camps, and in various ways to provide sustenance for the multitudes. In this order of government the following tribute was paid to the generosity which had been exhibited by certain Hindus : 'His Grace in Council has observed with much satisfaction the efforts made by all classes to relieve by private charity the existing distress among their fellow-townsmen. Conspicuous among these efforts are those of the Friend-in-Need Society, and His Grace, the Governor-in-Council resolves to grant to the Friend-in-Need Society a monthly donation equal to the special collections for relieving the poor, and to request the gentlemen above-mentioned to accept for distribution in food a monthly sum equal to the sum expended by them in feeding the poor, the only condition appended to these grants being that the money distributed for the government shall be applied to feeding those only who by age and infirmity

are incapable of laboring for their livelihood, and that
the establishments where the poor are fed shall be open
to the inspection of an officer deputed by the government.'

"Madras town relief thus passed, in December, 1876
into the hands of the police, who frequently had as many
as twenty thousand people daily to feed, and whose work
was done with a thoroughness beyond all praise. Thence-
forward, for nine months, only fugitive acts of charity,
save through the Friend-in-Need Society, were performed ;
the public, save as taxpayers, had no part or lot in the
efforts which were being made to save the perishing multitudes.

"What had happened in Madras was characteristic in a
measure of all the large towns in the presidency ; all were
crowded with infirm, sick, aged, and destitute poor. Attempts were made, unofficially, to relieve these. The
collector of North Arcot reports that at Arconum the
European railway officials and some of the native community 'subscribed handsomely' to provide a fund
whereby the poor might be fed daily. In Gudiathum,
also, the natives of their own accord, and without solicita-
tion or advice from European officials, established a relief
committee. In these places, however, as in many others,
the relief committees merely paved the way for the formation of relief camps, entirely supported by government
and under official control."

But neither the importation of grain by government
nor private charity was at all adequate to meet the exi-
gencies of the hour. The country might be full of rice,
but as the people had no money to buy, it was of little

use to them.   Hence government saw that relief works on
a large scale must be set on foot.   Some of these were
government works already under way, such as the Buckingham canal and unfinished railways; others were new
works started expressly to furnish employment to those
able to work.   Thus in August, 1877, there were on government relief works nine hundred and eighty-three thousand
five hundred and five, while those gratuitously relieved
were one million one thousand five hundred and eighty-
nine, making a total of one million nine hundred and
eighty-five thousand and ninety-four people fed by the
government of Madras alone.   In the Bombay Presidency
and the native States the same thing was going on.

To the credit of the government of India, both the
local and the supreme, it must be said that although it
was slow in waking up to the great emergency; and notwithstanding the tiresome, and as some thought, senseless
amount of "red tape" that had to be observed, yet it displayed an amount of energy and resource that was simply
marvelous, and in every way worthy of England's great
name.   Besides the relief works, government opened extensive relief camps all over the presidency.   These, of
course, were located in central places, so that while vast
multitudes of the helpless men, women, and children,
were thus saved, there were still other multitudes far beyond the reach of those camps, that must have perished
had not private charity come to the aid of government in
saving life.

As soon as it became evident that the northeast monsoon had failed, and that a famine was inevitable, some of
our missionaries, and notably Mr. Clough, sent out ap-

peals to England, America, and Burma for aid. To these appeals many generous responses came, and we were thus enabled in some degree to relieve a large number till the Mansion House fund became available. The first response received at Nellore was one hundred pounds from Deacon Wilbur, of Boston. Among the first forms of relief at Nellore was the organization of a "relief camp" on a small scale, in the mission compound, for the care of starving children, under the superintendence of Mrs. Downie, and at the expense of Mr. Grose, collector of the district. In this way nearly a hundred children were fed daily, and most of them preserved alive.

In addition to gifts and loans from personal friends, Mr. Clough took a contract to cut some four miles of the Buckingham canal as a relief work for the Christians of the Ongole field and their friends. By this means, hundreds and thousands were saved from starvation and death. The engineer in charge complimented Mr. Clough for the manner in which his work was done. He said : "Of the thirty-five miles under my charge your portion of the canal is the best."

To W. Digby, Esq., then editor of the "Madras Times," belongs the honor of suggesting the Mansion House fund, one of the most gigantic pieces of spontaneous charity the world has ever seen. By his persistent efforts in the face of considerable indifference, and even opposition, but warmly supported by many leading gentlemen in Madras, and notably Sir William Robinson, a meeting was held August 4, 1876, at which His Grace, the Governor, presided. The object of the meeting was to consider the propriety of soliciting aid from England. Resolutions were adopted, and a telegram prepared and forwarded to the Lord Mayors of London, York, Manchester, Dublin, Glasgow, Edinburgh, etc., asking for immediate aid, as the distress was great.

When the appeal reached England, the *London Times* took the matter up, and warmly advocated it. The Mansion House fund was opened, and the first list published contained two donations of one thousand pounds each, and two of five hundred pounds.

In the meantime a central committee had been formed in Madras, consisting of twenty-five gentlemen, of which Sir William Robinson was chosen chairman and Mr. William Digby, honorary secretary.

From this central committee a deputation was appointed to visit every district and organize local committees. As this required considerable time, and people were starving and dying all around, the missionaries at Nellore, Ongole, Ramapatam, and Kurnool, were appointed its agents for distributing relief in their respective districts.

When the relief committee was formed at Ongole, the Rev. J. E. Clough was appointed its honorary secretary and treasurer. In his report to the mission, Mr. Clough wrote: "Messrs. Williams, Loughridge, and Newhall have assisted us. Altogether we have paid out, in sums of from a few pices to six rupees, nearly twenty thousand rupees. Besides this princely sum we have also received handsome sums from friends in Burma, Assam, Siam, Bengal, England, and America, all of which have been disbursed as requested by the donors."

The Nellore committee was organized with J. Grose, Esq., Collector of Nellore, as chairman, and the Rev. D.

Downie, as honorary secretary and treasurer. For the relief of Nellore town, eight sub-committees were appointed, whose duty it was to visit every family, ascertain the distress, and fix upon a weekly dole of money. Lists were prepared, and according to these lists the doles were paid every week. A similar committee was appointed for each of the Talugs, but in these, relief was given in a lump sum to each family according to its needs. Sometimes it was for food, sometimes for seed grain, house-repairs, walls, etc. Besides the general work of secretary and treasurer, the missionary was chairman of one of the sub-committees.

A famine in India means total ruin to that large and industrious class, the small farmers, who depend upon the cultivation of their little patches of land for a living. Not only did they suffer from the loss of their crops, but by 1877 many of them had lost their cattle also. For a time the poor cattle were kept alive on weeds, leaves, prickly-pear, etc., and finally the thatch of the people's huts was taken from the houses and given them. In many cases the cattle were sent adrift to find food as they could, or given away to any one who would feed them. For this class, the form of relief usually was a sum of money for the purchase of seed-grain or bullocks or to dig a well, and to re-cover their huts.

Another large class that was among the first to suffer and the last to recover from the effects of the famine was comprised of the weavers and shoemakers. The weavers, especially, were great sufferers. There were six hundred thousand of them, exclusive of families in the presidency, and their condition speedily became very bad. All custom

was gone and they were literally without the means of securing a livelihood. In Nellore, we purchased for this class
ten thousand rupees' worth of thread, which was woven
into cloths and brought into the town. For their work
they received about one-half more than the usual rate
and this was all the relief they obtained. Of the many
thousands of cases in which the writer advanced money
or thread, he does not remember a single one in which
the cloths were not returned. These cloths were usually
distributed to the destitute women and children.

At one time, when fever was raging, ten thousand
blankets were purchased and distributed at an expense of
ten thousand rupees. Large quantities of quinine and
febrifuge were bought and distributed. For months the
mission house and compound seemed more like a mer-
chant's establishment than a mission.

In Nellore, two day nurseries were opened under the
supervision of Mrs. Grose, Mrs. Simpson, and Mrs.
Downie. Two meals a day were served to emaciated and
starving children, and women who had babies. In each
of these nurseries some four hundred children were fed
daily for seven months. Among the many forms of
relief, there were perhaps none that were so much needed,
none that were regarded with more favor, none more successful, and none more economically managed. The
average cost of feeding a child was about eight pices or
two cents a day. The average death rate was also smaller
than almost anywhere else. A few were too far gone
when admitted to recover, but the great majority were
preserved alive. It was a heart-touching sight to see the
poor little skeletons as they appeared when first brought

in. A few spoonfuls of milk or cunjee was all that they could stand at first, but they soon were able to eat their accustomed rice and curry.

The Nellore committee received two grants aggregating two hundred and fifty thousand rupees. Of this sum the missionary distributed with his own hand direct to the people relieved thirty thousand rupees. In addition to this he received six hundred rupees through Mr. Digby from the Baptists of England, seven hundred rupees from the "Merrill fund," Boston, and many smaller sums through the Society's treasurer, from personal friends in America.

As a mission we do not claim to have been exceptional in our efforts to save life and relieve distress. When in 1877 the Government of India said: "We say that human life should be saved at any cost and effort," we believe no body of men entered more heartily into that sentiment than the missionaries. At the closing meeting of the central committee in Madras, Mr. Digby said: "Among the most valued agents of the committee have been the missionaries of all creeds who have been, in many cases, the only available means by which the suffering could be reached. In some cases several months have been devoted exclusively to this work, and the missionaries have lived for weeks together among the people, traveling from village to village personally inquiring into cases of distress and relieving wants with their own hands."

It is difficult to estimate the actual cost of the famine. The loss of revenue was of course enormous, but how far that has been recovered we have no means of knowing.

The government expended in relief works eleven million pounds; but how far the money thus expended was on necessary and hence profitable works that will eventually repay their cost, we do not know.   But the receipts and expenditures of the Mansion House fund, which was a pure gratuitous charity, we know.

The total subscriptions from England, Scotland, Australia, and other Colonies, were six hundred and seventy-eight thousand five hundred and twelve pounds; from India, twenty-six thousand and twenty-six rupees, making a grand total of seven million nine hundred and seventy-nine thousand three hundred and fifty rupees.   And yet with all this expenditure, and the humane efforts of those engaged in distributing the relief, more than three million human beings perished either directly of starvation or from diseases caused by the famine.

It has often been said that the natives are strangers to the sense of gratitude.   No one who engaged in famine relief and who values truth will say so.   On this point the Rev. T. P. Adolphus says: " On the part of the recipients of the bounty, the most heartfelt expressions of gratitude have been addressed to me, and every possible outward token, indicative of the inward feeling, exhibited both by Hindu and by Mussulman, by male as well as by female."

It was a native gentleman who at the closing meeting in Madras said : " On behalf of my countrymen generally, and on behalf of the distressed famine-stricken of South India especially, to whom English charity came like sweet water to men dying of thirst, whose drooping spirits —nay, ebbing life were resuscitated by the timely and

kindly help, and enabled them to preserve themselves
and their children, to rebuild their huts, to sow their
fields and reap a harvest when they despaired of living
to see another—on behalf of millions of such of my
countrymen, I now express their most grateful thanks."

CHAPTER X.

THE GREAT INGATHERING.

The famine and accessions. Mr. Clough's canal contract. Combining work with Christian teaching. Effect upon the coolies. The influence of helpfulness. Baptisms deferred Larger accessions. One day's baptisms. Reasonableness of the pentecostal addition. Doubts expressed as to this Telugu ingathering. Mr. Clough's views. Delay of converts seemingly impossible. Efforts to keep them back. These unsuccessful. Baptism alone asked for by the multitudes. The request acceded to. In the Ramapatam field. The famine relief funds not alone the procuring cause. The movement of God. Departure of Mrs. Clough and her children from Ongole. Her efficiency. A destructive cyclone. Devastation at Ongole. Energetic restoration. Royal visitors. Native steadfastness. Mr. Clough's testimony thereto.

IT is useless to deny that there was a very close connection between the famine and the large accessions which followed it. We do not say that the relation was that of cause and effect, for in that case we should have to account for the fact that in many places there was the cause but no corresponding effect. But that the famine was one of the links in the chain of causes, we have no more doubt than we have that the famine in Egypt was one of the steps in Joseph's elevation to the governorship, and his consequent blessing to his own people.

The simple facts in the case were these: In addition to the distribution of famine relief funds all over his field, amounting to one hundred thousand dollars more or less, Mr. Clough took a contract to cut three and one-half miles of the Buckingham canal, which government was digging as a famine relief work. Mr. Clough's sole

109

object in undertaking this work was to find employment
for his Christians and other poor people in his field.
Quitting all other work for the time, he appointed his
preachers, teachers, colporteurs, and others, as his overseers.
During the intervals of rest these preachers gathered the
people together and preached to them about the great
salvation.   In this work the missionary encouraged them
and engaged himself as far as he could find time.   Thus
for months thousands of coolies were brought into close
contact with Christians of their own class, with the
preachers from whom many of them had no doubt heard
the gospel for years in their own villages, and with the
missionary who they knew was striving to save their
bodies from starvation as well as their souls from death.
The coolies were frequently changed.   Some, after gathering a few rupees, would start off to their villages and
others would take their places on the work.   And thus it
came about that a great many thousands were brought
under this influence of Christianity, and at a time when
they were peculiarly susceptible to its influence.   Now
what wonder if, under such circumstances, multitudes
were impressed with the truths of Christianity?   They
saw that Christians gave freely of their money to save
them from starvation.   They had never received such
treatment from their Hindu countrymen, and especially
from the Brahmans, who were their religious teachers.
But now they saw, chief of all, the missionary distributing relief everywhere and to all classes alike who needed
help.   What wonder if their conclusion was that the
religion which leads men to act so must be true?
   But to avoid receiving members into the church with

History of the Telugu Mission.
GUNDLACUMMA RIVER, WHERE 2,222 WERE BAPTIZED IN ONE DAY.

no higher motives than the pecuniary benefits referred to, all applications for baptism were denied during the fifteen months in which the missionary and his assistants were engaged in relief work. Not till all this was ended, and there was no more hope of any further relief, were applications for baptism entertained. Then, however, the missionary and his assistants saw no reason why they should longer refuse to baptize those whom they believed God had saved. They therefore commenced baptizing on the sixteenth of June, and by the end of December had baptized on profession of their faith in Christ, nine thousand six hundred and six converts, making the total membership of the Ongole Church, twelve thousand and four.

The largest number baptized in any one day was two thousand two hundred and twenty-two, which comes so near to the three thousand added to the church on the day of Pentecost as to demand special mention. It was the third of July, 1878. The baptistery was the Gundlacumma river at a place called Velumpilly, on the Northern Trunk Road, about ten miles north of Ongole. There is no bridge, but a sort of causeway over which carts may pass when the water is not too deep. The river at the time was not full, but on either side of the causeway the water was sufficiently deep for the ordinance, and the candidates had to take but a step or two from the banks to reach the administrator. The examination of the candidates had been held on the previous days. The converts were arranged on the bank on both sides of the causeway and men appointed to lead them in and out of the water. At six o'clock in the morning, two ordained native preachers took their places in the water, one on either side of the causeway. Prayer was offered and the baptizing commenced. When these two administrators became tired, two others took their places, and they in turn were relieved by still other two. At eleven the work stopped for the usual mid-day meal and rest. It was resumed at two, and about five o'clock the two thousand two hundred and twenty-two converts had been "buried with Christ in baptism" by six men, only two of them officiating at the same time. It will thus be seen that it occupied the time of two men for about eight hours. Had the six officiated at the same time, it would have occupied about two hours and forty minutes. If six Telugu ministers can baptize two thousand two hundred and twenty-two converts in two hours and forty minutes, how long would it take twelve apostles to baptize three thousand under similar circumstances? Just one hour and forty minutes. Granting that the circumstances were not equally favorable, and that some had to go to one pool and some to others, is not this question of the time required too absurd to call for serious notice?

When the report of these large accessions got abroad there was, as might be expected, a good deal of surprise and doubt expressed as to the expediency of baptizing such crowds of poor, ignorant people, with little or no previous instruction, except that they had heard the gospel preached for a longer or shorter time. And to many it seemed especially hazardous to receive them so soon after the distribution of such large sums of famine relief money. But on the other hand, while Mr. Clough appears to have anticipated such doubts and objections, and appears to have made every possible effort to delay the baptisms,—

especially in large numbers,—yet he expresses the firmest conviction on the part of himself and his assistants that the converts were genuine believers, and that the work was of God. But on this point we shall let Mr. Clough speak for himself. In his annual report for 1878, after reviewing the "spiritual outlook" and the effect of the famine on the religious beliefs of the Hindus, the application of large numbers for baptism and of postponing them for fifteen months lest some might be seeking more money rather than spiritual blessings, he says:

"By the end of May we had closed the relief operations in Ongole and throughout this section, except for destitute orphans and for seed-grain to small ryots [farmers] who actually owned land, and probably without help could not procure seed. For fifteen months (from March 11, 1877, to June 16, 1878,) we had not baptized a single person. Some here in Ongole, and about Ongole, whom I had known personally for ten or twelve years, I was fully convinced were new creatures in Christ Jesus, and it seemed to me duty to baptize them. I felt that I must, or fail to please Jesus. June 16th we "raised the gate"; but, when it was up, we found it impossible, according to our sense of duty, to shut it down again. In fact, to own the truth, I feared to do so. I felt that those whom I, or trustworthy assistants and well-known church-members, had known for months or longer, and who gave evidence that they had not only left idolatry, but also believed in Jesus as their Saviour, must be baptized, or that I must throw up my commission, and get out of the way: of course, I had no idea of doing either. I only wanted to keep the multi-

II

tude of converts off two or three months longer, that all
the friends of missions might be free from doubts, although
personally, I had been convinced for above a year that the
work was of God. But to delay was impossible, for God's
time had fully come to glorify himself.

"The first Sunday in July was to be our bi-monthly
meeting; but I wished to keep as many out of Ongole as
I could. Small-pox was prevalent in many villages. The
tom-toms had been beaten time and again, by order
of government officials, warning all villagers to go to
their homes, as neither government nor the Mansion
House committee could do any more for them. The town
was very dirty, and the fear of small-pox or epidemic
cholera was considerable: hence I wrote letters, and sent
them to all the native preachers, telling them to leave the
wives and children at home, not to allow a single Christian, unless now and then one or two of the leading members who had urgent requests to make, to come with
them, and to meet me at Velumpilly, the first station north
of Ongole, on the Gundlacumma river, ten miles distant. ·
I told them the fear Ongoleans were in, and that in the
villages on the way small-pox was very bad, etc.: hence
this order I had given them would, if obeyed, result in
good only, while to disregard it might scatter this con-
tagious disease far and wide, and cause the death of
many. Notwithstanding my letters and the efforts of the
preachers, the converts would not stop behind. As soon
as the preacher had been gone a few hours, the converts
up and followed.

"The first preachers that arrived at Velumpilly wrote
to me that they had done their best to follow the requests

made in my circular, but that the converts had not obeyed them, but were coming in crowds from every side. I hastened off, and hoped to get most to go back to their homes for the present. It could not be done without taking too much responsibility. The multitude one and all said, through their leading men and preachers, 'We don't want any money ; we will not ask you for any, either directly or indirectly, either now or hereafter.' Only a few had ever been assisted, except by their pay for their work when on the canal ; and said they, 'As we have lived thus far by our work,—by the blisters on our hands we can prove this to you,—so we will continue to live, or, if we die, we shall die ; but we want you to baptize us.'

"We held a special service ; and, after much prayer and consideration, we decided to baptize any and all who had given to the preachers evidence extending over some months that they were Christians, and who had an intelligent understanding of the main facts of the Christian religion. The evidence of the preachers, with that of the leading members of the church in their localities who had been baptized years ago, or other reliable information concerning their change of heart, was decided to be sufficient. The result was the baptism of three thousand five hundred and thirty-six in three days."

In the Ramapatam field, lying between Ongole and Nellore, there was no such general movement, yet over six hundred were baptized during the same time. In Nellore, where almost as much relief work was done by the missionary as was done at Ongole, excepting the canal contract, the movement was scarcely felt. This is significant, and goes against the idea that it was wholly a result

of the famine. The famine may have been and probably
was the immediate cause of this great movement, just as
the financial crisis in the United States in 1857 was the immediate cause of the great revival that swept all over the
land. But we prefer to say that God used not only the
famine, but the preaching and the praying and the whole
combination of circumstances, to lead the people to cast
away their idols, embrace the new religion, and devote
their lives to the service of the living God.

Perhaps the most memorable event in the Ongole
Station in 1879, was the departure of Mrs. Clough and her
children for America. After five of the most trying years
in the history of the mission, Mrs. Clough's health broke
down, and it became evident to all that she must return
home, if her life was to be preserved. All through the
terrible famine, and the subsequent and almost equally
terrible siege of cholera, Mrs. Clough stood resolutely at
her post, ministering to the famished and plague-stricken
people, and in her own quiet but effectual manner, assisting her husband in every good word and work. It is no
disparagement to Mr. Clough to say that much of his
grand success was due to the faithful and devoted helpmeet he had in Mrs. Clough. Mr. Clough accompanied
his family as far as England, leaving Madras May 13th,
and after seeing them safely on board a steamer for New
York, returned to his work, reaching Ongole on the 15th
of August.

During Mr. Clough's absence, the station was in charge
of Rev. W. B. Boggs, who arrived in Madras, January
18, 1879, and proceeded direct to Ongole, and successfully
carried on the work till Mr. Clough's return.

In November, a destructive cyclone visited Ongole, doing much damage to the mission property. Mr. Clough,
believing the monsoon to be over, had started on an evangelistic tour expecting to be gone a month. He had
reached his second halting place, some fifteen miles north
of Ongole, when the cyclone reached him. It was on the
19th, about one o'clock in the morning. By three o'clock
the wind was terrific and the rain came down in torrents.
Trees were torn up by the roots, or broken off, and the
branches were flying about in all directions. The tent
was in danger of being torn to pieces, so it was hastily let
down, and left in the rain and mud, while Mr. Clough
and his helpers betook themselves to a village near by,
where they found refuge in a cow shed where they remained till the morning of the 20th. They succeeded in
repitching the tent, and were getting their clothes dried
and things set to rights, when a messenger from Mr. Boggs
came announcing a terrible state of affairs at Ongole.
This decided Mr. Clough to return to Ongole at once.

It was sad to see the work of so many years destroyed
in a few hours. Most of the school dormitories and
native houses were either destroyed or badly injured.
Many of the shade trees were blown down, and altogether
the two Ongole compounds presented a sorry sight. But
like many another calamity it might have been a great
deal worse. There was nothing to be done but clear up
the place and rebuild as fast as possible.

It is not often that missionaries are favored with royal
visitors, but in January, 1880, the Duke of Buckingham,
cousin of Queen Victoria, then Governor of Madras, visited the Nellore District. While in Nellore a visit to the

mission had been arranged, but was broken up by a supposed case of small-pox in the compound. At Ongole,
however, a visit was paid to the mission, which was much
enjoyed both by the royal party and the missionaries.
Before leaving, His Grace seeing the devastation that
had been made by the cyclone asked permission to rebuild two of the dormitories, and handed Mr. Boggs a
check for four hundred rupees for the purpose.

No one expected that of all the vast multitude
gathered into the church since 1878 there would be none
who would fall away. Indeed, the wonder would be that
in such a harvest there were not a good many tares
gathered with the wheat. But according to the testimony of the missionary the tares seem to have been very
few indeed. The following extract from a letter written
by Mr. Clough, dated April 1, 1880, will show how he
found the Christians whose villages he visited two years
after the baptisms : " On account of the famine and
multiplicity of station work after the ingathering of 1878,
the itinerating work of the Ongole field had been neglected. On the 17th of January I started on an evangelistic tour. I was absent from Ongole just two months.
I visited ninety-eight villages where our people live ; saw
delegates from perhaps one hundred other villages and
baptized one thousand and sixty-eight persons on profession of their faith in Christ. I never had such
hearing before . . . . In five or six villages the Christians were doing badly. In one village five persons were
excluded for contracting infant marriages. In two villages two were excluded for adultery ; and in another
village eleven were excluded because they confessed that

they had deceived us when they were baptized . . . . In all the other villages we felt daily that the need of more preachers and teachers was great, and that for the want of teaching the Christians had fallen into some errors in some places . . . . On the whole, I fully believe that the great mass of converts are living as well as they know, and that after we are able to teach them more fully and give them pastors, they will become strong men and women in Christ Jesus."

This is certainly an excellent testimony from one who knows the field and the people as no other man does. Even after making all due allowance for the fact that these people cling to Mr. Clough as children to a father, and that he exerts over them a powerful and magnetic influence, it is simply marvelous that after two years of very imperfect watchcare so few had to be excluded from such a vast mass of poor, ignorant Christians.

CHAPTER XI.

RESULTS OF THE GREAT REVIVAL.

An interesting incident. An eventful service. Ordination of native preachers. Excellence of the candidates. Sermon by Mr. Downie. Parts performed by native preachers. Accession to the mission of Mr. and Mrs. Manley. Death of "Obulu." Dr. S. F. Smith's visit. A demand for schools. Christianity compelling schools. Establishment of schools in the Ongole field. The Ongole High School. Mr. Manley's report. Difficult examinations. Success of candidates. The staff of teachers. The arrangement of primary instruction. Different classes of scholars. The needs of the school. The Christian influence of the school. Elevation of the school to the grade of a college. The vastness of the Ongole field. The field divided. New stations. A trip to the United States for Dr. Clough. Presenting the mission's needs. Early death of Mr. and Mrs. Rayl. The work of the woman's society at Ongole. Other large accessions. Death of Mr. Edward A. Kelly. Dr. Mabie's visit again. Baptisms by him and his companion. The accessions mainly from the non-caste Madigas. Tendency of other classes toward Christianity. Probability of increase in the movement. The caste people. Rest for Dr. Clough. Helpers during his absence. An additional force for the high school. Suggestions as to the work at Ongole. Danger of unworthy motives. False influences among the Christians. Possible disaster through change of leaders. Need of doctrinal training. Another subdivision of the mission needed. Reorganization of the churches. A larger staff of missionaries. Responsibility of the home churches.

NEXT to the baptism of two thousand two hundred and twenty-two converts on a single day, the most interesting incident in connection with the great ingathering was the ordination of twenty-four native ministers on the 16th of April, 1880. The following account of it is given by Mr. Boggs: "According to appointment the preachers, teachers, helpers, Bible-women, etc., connected with the Ongole mission, assembled here on Saturday,

120

the 10th inst., at the regular quarterly meeting. They had not been in since the latter part of December, and there was much of interest to report and to hear.

"On Sunday, April 11th, a very large congregation gathered to commemorate the Saviour's death, and to hear the word of truth. There were probably not less than a thousand persons present. Mr. Clough preached from Gen. 18 : 14, 'Is anything too hard for the Lord?' The afternoon was devoted to the examination of candidates for baptism ; the preachers under whose labors these people had heard and believed the gospel were all present, and gave evidence concerning them all. The result was that one hundred and eighty-seven were received, and at 6 P. M., I baptized them. The next day seventeen more were received, and were baptized in the evening by Bro. Price, making one thousand two hundred and ninety-five baptized in the Ongole field since January 1.

"It had been felt for some time that a considerable number of the native preachers connected with this station were worthy of full recognition as ministers of the gospel. It also seemed evident that the time had arrived for the organization of separate churches in all the important places where the number of disciples was sufficient to justify it ; and on this account also the ordination of these men seemed desirable. In response to a call from the Ongole Church, a council convened at Ongole, April 14–16, to consider the propriety of formally setting apart to the work of the gospel ministry a number of native preachers laboring in this field. Rev. D. Downie of Nellore, and Rev. R. R. Williams of Ramapatam, with native delegates from each place, were present, besides the Ongole missionaries and native brethren. There were previously seven ordained native preachers in the Ongole field. The council was organized by the choice of Bro. Williams as moderator, and M. Ezra (ordained native preacher) as clerk.

"The examination was close and deliberate, and occupied two days and a half. It embraced, as usual, the important points of conversion and call to the ministry, and an outline of Christian doctrine ; many testing questions were asked both by the missionaries and native delegates. and the answers were generally very satisfactory. Their knowledge of Christian doctrine seemed surprising, especially after hearing each one of them, in relating his experience, speak of the time, only a few years back, when he was worshiping idols, and was in utter ignorance of the true God and the way of life.

"The result was that twenty-four of the best, most experienced, and successful preachers connected with the Ongole station were considered worthy of the confidence implied in this act of public recognition. They are men who for years have faithfully, consistently, zealously, and with abundant fruits proclaimed the gospel of Jesus, and cared for the flocks over which they have been placed. Several of them have enjoyed the advantage of a four years' course at the seminary at Ramapatam. These men will continue to labor in the same fields where they have already been so useful, and continue to feed the flocks which have been gathered largely through their instrumentality.

"A large congregation assembled in the spacious Ongole chapel on the afternoon of the 16th. Mr. Downie

preached the ordination sermon from 1 Tim. 4 : 15,
'Meditate upon these things; give thyself wholly to them;
that thy profiting may appear to all.' It was a condensed
discourse, containing much truth in few words. Mr.
Williams delivered an earnest charge, in which he addressed both the people and the candidates on their
respective responsibilities and duties. Then the twenty-
four all knelt, and the hands of the presbytery were laid
on them while the ordaining prayer was offered by Rev.
N. Canakiah of Nellore; after which the benediction was
pronounced by Yerragoontla Periah, the oldest man
among those just ordained, and the spiritual father of a
multitude of children."

At the beginning of the year the Rev. W. I. Price
arrived from America to join the mission, but after a
few months he retired from this station, feeling that duty
called him to labor elsewhere. The vacancy, however,
was soon supplied by the arrival in August of the Rev.
W. R. Manley and wife, from Burma, who had been
connected with the Telugu mission work in Rangoon for
the previous six months. M. Obulu, "a good minister of
Jesus Christ," was called to his rest September 5th. His
death was a great loss to the Ongole field.

On the 8th of March, 1881, after visiting Nellore,
Alloor, and Ramapatam, Dr. S. F. Smith and Mrs.
Smith, paid a visit to Ongole. As in the case of Nellore,
we refer our readers for an account of this visit to Dr.
Smith's "Rambles in Mission Fields."

While evangelistic work has ever held the first place
in the policy of the mission, and we trust will always

continue to do so, education undoubtedly deserves the
second. Following the great ingathering a demand
sprang up for schools. Ignorance and Christianity are
diametrically opposed. Education does not necessarily
make a community Christian, but a Christian community invariably demands education. There are thousands
of villages in India which have schools and no Christians,
but very few Christian villages, if any, which have no
school. To meet this demand on the Ongole field a large
number of schools were established. In 1877, the number of village schools was forty-two. This was increased
to eighty-three in 1878, and later the number was one
hundred and seventy-six schools with two thousand one
hundred pupils. The station schools were also largely
increased, and made more efficient. The mi.sion high
school was opened in May, 1880, under Mr. Edward A.
Kelly as head master. In this year, the Rev. W. R.
Manley, who had been laboring among the Telugus of
Rangoon was transferred to Ongole, and in August, 1881,
was appointed to the principalship of the high school.

The aim and work of this high school may be gathered
from Mr. Manley's report of 1882, from which we quote
as follows: "This institution, although located in
Ongole, is intended to meet the entire wants of the Telugu
mission, so far as higher education is concerned, just as
the seminary at Ramapatam does in the matter of theological training. It is not merely the only one in the
Telugu mission: it is the only institution of the kind
between Nellore and Guntur. The curriculum of studies
is that prescribed by the Madras University. It embraces
a course of seven years' study, and is so arranged as to

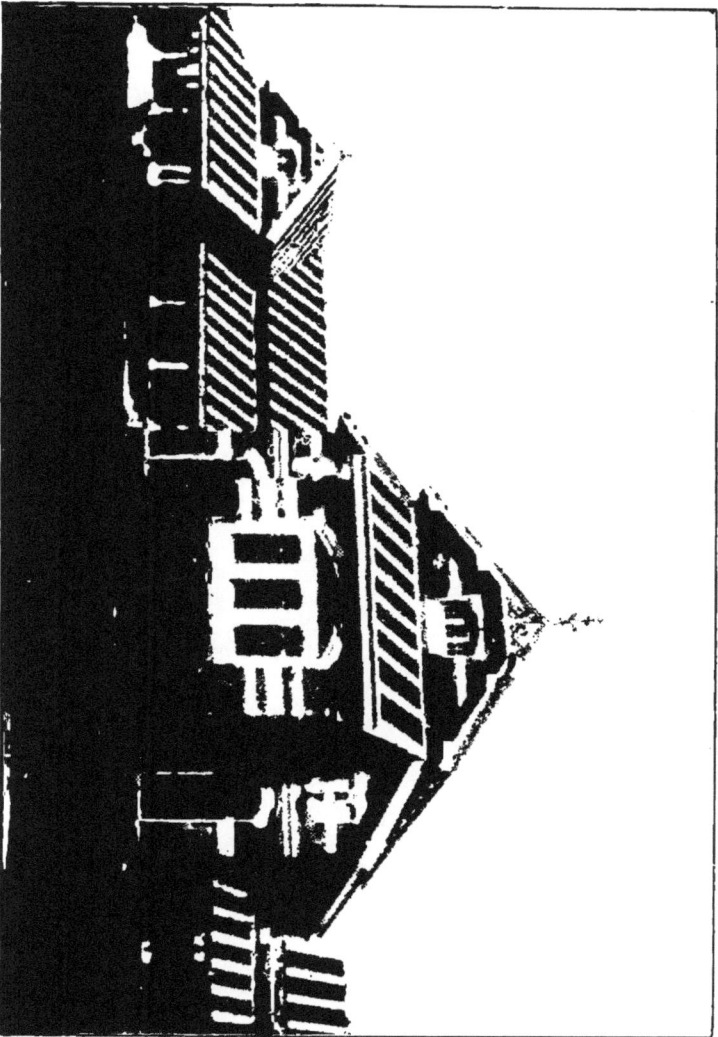

MISSION HIGH SCHOOL, ONGOLE.

give a native student, in addition to a knowledge of the grammar and literature of his own language, a fair English education. The vernacular is retained throughout the entire course, but English becomes the language of the text-book and recitation after the third year. The very patent reason for this is, that it is only through the medium of some other language than their own, that any education, in the proper sense of the term, can be given to these people. The Bible forms a regular part of the course in all except the two lowest classes.

"There are two very difficult examinations; one at the end of the fifth year, by the government, termed the middle school examination, which makes the successful candidate eligible to employment in the government civil service; and the other at the end of the seventh year, by the Madras University, termed the matriculation examination. This year a class of fifteen boys was prepared for the middle school, and one of nine for the matriculation examination. Of the former, all passed but three, four of them being in the first grade. Of the latter, only three passed; but as this is as good as the average for the entire Nellore District, it is not quite so discouraging as might at first appear.

"The staff of teachers embraces, in addition to the principal, two Eurasian, and six native teachers. There is also an alphabet class connected with the school, though not really a part of it, for the benefit of our Christian boys and others who are not prepared to enter the first class. There have been opened also two primary schools—one in Ongole, and the other at Kottapatam, ten miles east of Ongole—to serve as feeders for the high school. There are fifty or sixty boys in these two schools, many of whom will come into the high school as soon as they are prepared.

"Among our students there are Brahmans, Sudras, and Mohammedans, besides our Christian boys. No distinctions of caste or religion are allowed; but all these different classes sit together on the same bench, and recite the same lessons. The school has grown to such an extent that there is not sufficient room in the present house. There is also great need of books of reference and apparatus.

"There have been during the year, including the alphabet class, one hundred and seventy-eight boys enrolled, with an average monthly attendance of one hundred and forty-six. Of these, according to their religions, fifty-four were Christians, almost all of whom have been baptized, seven were Mohammedans, and one hundred and seventeen were Hindus."

While Dr. Clough was at home in 1891, he presented a petition to the Executive Committee requesting that the high school be raised to the grade of a college, and that fifty thousand dollars be provided for its endowment. Believing that such a college would be needed in the near future for our Christian boys, and at the same time wishing to take advantage of Dr. Clough's presence in the country to raise the funds, the Committee granted the request with the understanding that the money should be collected in such a way as not to interfere with the ordinary contributions to the Union. The money was secured, and the college will be opened when there are Christian students to enter it. Non-Christians will, of course, be admitted to its benefits, but it is understood that the college is primarily for our Christian young men.

At the close of 1882, the number of church-members belonging to the Ongole field was twenty thousand eight hundred and sixty-five. Nominally, these were divided into twenty-seven churches, but practically they were all under the management of the missionaries at Ongole, and it was far too large a body of Christians, and scattered over far too large a territory to be successfully worked from one station. A division of the field was therefore necessary, and this was happily accomplished previous to Dr. Clough's return to America. The new stations were—Cumbum, about sixty miles west of Ongole; to this station the Rev. W. B. Boggs and wife were appointed; Vinukonda, about sixty miles northwest of Ongole, to which Rev. G. N. Thomssen and wife were appointed; Nursaraopett, fifty-five miles northeast of Ongole, to which Rev. R. Maplesden and wife were appointed; and Bapatla, forty-five miles northeast of Ongole, to which Rev. E. Bullard and wife were appointed. These new fields will be more fully referred to later on.

Dr. Clough left Ongole November 17, 1883, for a brief visit to his family in America. In view of the great work that had been accomplished in Ongole, Dr. Clough was welcomed home with great enthusiasm. He had scarcely touched his native land ere appeals came to him from all quarters to address meetings and give an account of the great work. After only eleven days with his family, he was summoned to New York to address a series of meetings in the interests of the Missionary Union, which at the time was sadly in need of largely increased contributions. It is needless to say that the meetings secured a large attendance, and that Dr. Clough's addresses were listened to with deep interest.

When the immediate necessities of the Union were met, Dr. Clough was permitted to present certain claims of the Telugu Mission. These were, first, two mission houses for Madras, and second, an extensive addition to the high school building. Both of these objects were accomplished.

During Dr. Clough's absence the station was in charge of Rev. D. K. Rayl, who arrived in Ongole August 16, 1882. When Mr. Rayl left New York he was to all appearance a strong, healthy man. The seeds of consumption must, however, have been in him, for soon after he reached India the disease began to make rapid progress, and in May, 1884, he quit India and set out for home, which he succeeded in reaching only to die. His wife survived him only twenty days, dying of the same disease.

Miss Emma Rauschenbusch, an appointee of the Woman's Society of the West, arrived in Madras November 30, 1882. Her original designation was to Ongole, but circumstances seemed to favor her remaining in Madras. The following year, however, the claims of Ongole were brought to bear on her, and she was induced to proceed to that station in July, 1883, and take charge of the boys' school and Bible woman's work. The Society of the West provided for her a handsome bungalow, a large boys' school, and a Bible woman's house, all of which were finished in 1885. Miss Rauschenbusch continued her work in Ongole till 1887, when her health broke down, and she was obliged to return home.

In 1890, another remarkable movement took place, resulting in the largest number of accessions since 1878. The quarterly meeting at Ongole was an unusually large one, and before it closed three hundred and sixty-three were baptized. The interest was unusually great, and as large numbers were reported ready for baptism, but who could not come to Ongole at that time, a second meeting was called for December 27th and 28th. On the latter day one thousand six hundred and seventy-one were baptized on profession of faith in Christ. By the first of March, 1891, this number was increased to four thousand and thirty-seven. At Cumbum some three thousand five hundred were baptized between October and March, and if we include the smaller numbers baptized in other fields the total accessions will not fall far short of the great ingathering of 1878.

A severe blow fell upon the Ongole field in the death of Mr. Edward A. Kelly, who entered the mission service first as the head master of the high school in 1880. Two years later he received an appointment in government service, but in 1888, he returned to the mission as an assistant to Dr. Clough. Here he did good and faithful service till called to his reward. He won the esteem and affection of all who knew him, and his death was a sore bereavement to his family and Dr. Clough, and a great loss to the mission.

We have already referred to Dr. Mabie's visit to Nellore and Ramapatam. From the latter place he went on to Ongole, where he spent two or three days looking into the work in and about the station. On Sunday, the 8th of February, Drs. Mabie and Waterman baptized

I

ninety-seven converts. On Monday, Dr. Clough and his visitors started across the country to strike the railway *en route* for Bombay. On the way they encamped at a village called Chandaloor, where they held a two days' meeting. Some twelve hundred people assembled in a grove, and listened attentively to the word preached. A large number professed faith in Christ, and of these Drs. Mabie and Waterman baptized five hundred and eighty-four, and on the following day one hundred and sixty more were baptized. These baptisms are included in the four thousand and thirty-seven referred to above.

Although this late movement is not confined to what is now the Ongole field, yet it is confined to what was the Ongold field in 1878. There is not a station in the mission that has not had more or less additions, but these large accessions have been almost exclusively from the same class of people, namely, the Madigas, and from the same region as those in 1878. This is a very significant fact, and should be considered in discussing the question of these "mass movements" toward Christianity. They indicate what may reasonably and confidently be expected when Christianity takes hold of the other great division of the non-caste people, the Malas, and also, though probably later, the people of the various castes. In other parts of the Telugu country, and in other missions, the Malas give evidence of such a disposition to move *en masse* toward Christianity. But so far, in our own mission, the indications of such a movement are not apparent, although our work in Nellore and elsewhere started with the Malas, and our converts generally have been from that class.

The work among the Madigas in the north and north-west of our mission has received such an impetus that in all probability it will go on, augmenting as it goes, till the whole class will come over to Christianity.   In the near future we fully believe a similar movement will take place among the Malas.   The caste people may be slower to move, but they too will certainly come.   Indeed, already in one field of our mission the caste people are believing even more readily than the non-castes of the same field.

One of the results of Dr. Mabie's visit to the Telugu mission was that he succeeded in convincing Dr. Clough that the time had come for him to retire from the field for a time and return home for needed recuperation and rest.   For some years it was evident to all but himself that he had reached that point where he was liable to utterly break down at any moment.   Moreover, it was thought that Dr. Clough could do better service to the mission by going home and exerting his influence in getting the new men that had been called for, than he could by staying on in his imperfect health.   Accordingly he left Ongole March 17th, and sailed from Bombay on the 28th.

The Rev. P. M. Johnson and wife, who were designated to Ongole, arrived there December 5, 1890.   Having so recently come to the country it was thought advisable to request the Rev. J. Heinrichs and wife to remove to Ongole and carry on the work till Dr. Clough's return. They had spent some fifteen months in Nellore, devoting most of their time to the study of Telugu.   They left Nellore March 20th to begin their new and difficult work at Ongole.

Prof. Lewis E. Martin and Rev. Oscar R. McKay arrived in Ongole in December, 1891. Mr. Martin was specially designated as principal of the high school, a work for which he was especially fitted, having held a similar position in Japan. But even for such a position, when most of the work is in English, it was deemed best to leave Mr. Martin free to study the language before assuming the duties of his position. In the event of the school becoming a college the expectation is that both Mr. Martin and Mr. McKay will devote themselves to that work.

We might linger at Ongole and give more details of all the wonderful work that has been accomplished in that fruitful field. But enough, we trust, has been said to give a fairly adequate view of the field, of the work accomplished, and of its still greater possibilities. Before leaving it, however, we may be permitted to offer a few suggestions as to the dangers to which Ongole is especially exposed, and the precautions which should be taken to avoid them.

In the first place, it must be admitted that when converts have come in such masses, and especially when they have come from the very lowest class of society, there is a likelihood that at least some of them were influenced by unworthy motives; and that others who without any desire to deceive, were borne on by the current of prevailing feeling, and baptized without any real conviction of sin or conversion to God. Hence church discipline should be exercised with the greatest care and vigor.

Secondly. As these converts are from the very lowest class of society, few of them being even able to read, they are in danger of being influenced not only by heathenism by which they are surrounded, but also by Roman Catholicism and other false forms of Christianity. Indeed, this very danger was one of the causes which precipitated the great movement in 1878. The Roman Catholics were not only ready to receive the converts, but two priests were on the ground planning to baptize them. But for God's interposition, and the skill and vigor Dr. Clough displayed in turning the movement in our direction, they would in all probability have gone over to the Romanists, and that would not only have been a curse to the converts, but would have been a serious hindrance to the progress of God's work in this district for all time. So long as Dr. Clough with his great influence and power remains on the field, this danger need cause no special alarm. But should he die, or be permanently removed from the mission, and a man with less ability to hold the people, or with different ideas of how mission work ought to be conducted take his place, a very little thing might create a panic which would prove disastrous. Hence it is of the greatest importance that these converts be thoroughly trained in the principles of our faith. To do this, the Ongole field ought again to be subdivided into three or four fields and a missionary placed in each.

Thirdly. The churches ought to be more thoroughly organized on the New Testament model. Nominally there are sixteen churches on the Ongole field, but ordinarily the ordinances and business of all the churches are attended to at Ongole just the same as before the village churches were set off. This is probably unavoidable, and will be till the field is again divided and a very much larger staff of missionaries is on the ground.

It remains for American Baptists to say whether these dangers are to remain or be averted. If men are supplied in sufficient numbers, there is practically no end to the numbers that will believe and join the Lord's hosts.

In October, 1892, thirteen men, married and single, sailed from Boston to join the mission. Of these, five or six will be stationed in different parts of the present Ongole field. As soon as they have acquired a working knowledge of the language new fields will be formed and thus, it is hoped, the dangers above referred to will be averted.

CHAPTER XII.

RAMAPATAM.

RAMAPATAM is a small village on the shore of the Bay of Bengal, forty-five miles north of Nellore. It is a place of no especial importance in itself, but previous to 1870 was the headquarters of the sub-collector of the district. In that year, however, the sub-collector was removed to Ongole. This left unoccupied a fine large compound of nearly a hundred acres and two bungalows all ready for occupation. As there was no prospect of any government official requiring the premises, the property was thrown into the market and offered at a comparatively small price.

It will be remembered that after the occupation of Ongole, Ramapatam was one of the places selected by the missionaries as the most desirable location for a station between Nellore and Ongole, and also that the Rev. A. V. Timpany and wife, who were to occupy the new station, were already in Nellore. Mr. Timpany had searched over the whole region for a suitable place for the station, but not one could be found. But as soon as he reached Nellore he heard of the proposed change of the sub-collectorate. Shortly afterward this magnificent property was purchased for the nominal sum of three thousand rupees. One of the bungalows was occupied by Mr. and Mrs. Timpany, February 5, 1870, and the other was speedily converted into a chapel, and thus the missionaries were enabled to begin their work at once.

On the 25th of March, a church was organized composed of members from the Nellore and Ongole churches and numbering thirty-five. This was increased to one hundred and fifteen by the close of the year. There would probably have been a much larger number received, but a spirit of persecution broke out and many of the Christians were shamefully treated. This led some to turn back, and others who manifested a disposition to renounce heathenism were deterred. The immediate cause of this persecution was the refusal of the Christians of Kondiahpalem to eat meat sacrificed to idols.

Mr. Timpany shared very largely the faith of Messrs. Day, Jewett, and Clough, respecting the conversion of large numbers of Telugus in the very near future. The genuineness of his faith was evident in the manner and character of his life and work. He believed the heathen were dying, and the sincerity of his faith was seen in the way he devoted his life to save them.

Miss Peabody, the first single lady sent to this mission, arrived in Ramapatam in 1872. After two years of study and prospecting as to how and where she should begin work for the women and girls for whom she had come to labor, she decided that a girls' boarding school presented the best field. This was probably wise, and it certainly was safe, since it had been found to work successfully both in Nellore and Ongole. Accordingly, a building was prepared and a school begun with six girls. In 1875, the number had increased to forty-five.

In 1877, Miss Peabody became the wife of the Rev. Geo. Pearce, a retired missionary of the English Baptist Missionary Society, and then living at Ootacamund, on the Neilgiri Hills. This, however, did not end Miss Peabody's missionary career. Mr. Pearce still had much missionary zeal, and although himself unfamiliar with the Tamil, he had gathered a company of Tamils at Ootacamund and employed a native catechist to preach to them. He also had an English congregation. Into this service Mrs. Pearce entered earnestly.

By the end of the fifth year of the new station at Ramapatam two churches had been organized, with a total membership of seven hundred and sixty-nine; two station schools, a number of village schools, and seven out-stations established. The confidence of the heathen had been secured. At first the missionary was regarded as an enemy and shunned, now he was everywhere warmly welcomed as a friend. All classes came in crowds to hear him preach. Mr. Timpany had some knowledge of medicine which, besides enabling him to relieve much suffering, was a great help in securing the confidence of the people. The caste people at first refused to take medicine mixed with water, but finding it was that or nothing, they soon laid aside their prejudice and received the remedy.

Mr. and Mrs. Timpany returned to America in February, 1876. During the two years he was at home, Mr. Timpany studied medicine and took the degree of M. D. Being a Canadian he was urged to leave our mission and join that of the Canadian Board. This caused him a good deal of anxious thought and it was only after a severe struggle that he finally felt compelled to join the mission of his own country. He loved his old field at Ramapatam, but felt that duty called him to Cocanada. Here he labored earnestly and faithfully until the 19th of February, 1885, when he was seized with cholera and in a few hours entered into his eternal rest.

The Rev. A. A. Newhall joined the mission in 1875, and succeeded Mr. Timpany at Ramapatam. It was a most unfortunate time for a young and inexperienced missionary to have thrust upon him the care and responsibility of a large mission station. The great famine was just impending, and instead of having the first year or two for study and getting acquainted with the field and people, he had to lend a hand in the one great work of the hour, famine relief.

When the Timpanys left, Miss Peabody accompanied them to Madras and remained there about eight months studying medicine. Miss Mary A. Wood, who had been appointed to Nellore and who arrived there in January, 1875, was requested to take temporary charge of the girls' school at Ramapatam till Miss Peabody returned. But in the meantime she became Mrs. Newhall, and on Miss Peabody's return, Mrs. Newhall handed over to her the girls' school while she took charge of the boys' school and otherwise entered earnestly into the work of the station. But her missionary life was brief. She died in Nellore, October 9, 1877.

The reader will scarcely have failed to observe that we have presented the great ingathering of 1878 in its most favorable aspects. But it would not be historically correct to leave on the reader's mind the impression that all the missionaries were equally sanguine with reference to the movement. That God's Spirit was moving multitudes to believe and turn to Christ no one for a moment doubted; but that large numbers of the heathen were seeking, not Christ but the missionary, his influence and merely temporal good, several were disposed to fear if not to believe. The following from one of Mr. Newhall's letters will show that he shared to some extent this fear, while at the same time a genuine work of the Holy Spirit was in progress, which his own field to some extent shared.

" The distribution of so much relief money, while it has saved multitudes of lives, has also awakened in the people a desire, so natural to them at all times, but now intensified, to make all the gain possible out of their relations to white people. Deception, fraud, and dishonesty have been practiced by the heathen, and, I am sorry to say, by a few of the so-called Christians, and have diverted many a rupee from the end for which it was sent out and given. This fact made the work of distributing relief money very difficult, and now opposes a great obstacle to the prosecution of mission work : that is, *such* mission work as all intelligent friends of missions delight in. But there has also been awakened, evidently by the Holy Spirit, a desire to embrace a religion that exhibits such fruits of love and benevolence in such marked contrast with the cruelty and selfishness of heathenism. God has seemed to make this recent benevolence of the English and American people an entering wedge for the gospel in multitudes of cases where the evidences of true conversion are clear and satisfactory. The difficulties of the present ingathering are in the cases of multitudes who seem to have mixed motives for desiring baptism : and some of them are of the most puzzling character. Some after answering the usual questions satisfactorily, on being asked what advantage it is going to be to believe in Christ and join the church, will frankly confess that it will bring them clothes and food and the favor of the missionary."

During 1878 there were five hundred and twenty-six baptized on the Ramapatam field. The station schools were continued, but with great difficulty, after Mrs. Newhall's death. It is of the greatest importance that every station should have a missionary family. A man without a wife is badly handicapped in such work. Still, the work of the year was on the whole very prosperous, and for that very reason it is all the more painful to record the utter collapse of the Ramapatam mission field in 1879.

Up to 1878 there had been but one church at Ramapatam
for the Christians generally and the students of the seminary. But during the great revival a large number of
converts had been gathered by the teachers and students
of the seminary. At first, these converts were baptized
into the station church. But as the number increased,
questions arose respecting their reception, which led to
the formation of an independent seminary church. This
led to further complications which greatly marred the
peace and harmony of the station.

Previous to his departure for the United States, Mr.
Drake invited Mr. Newhall to leave Ramapatam and
take charge of the Kurnool field. This Mr. Newhall
was not altogether willing to do, but was willing to undertake the care of both fields till help should come from
home. But owing to the great distance between the two
fields, this was an almost impossible task. He, however,
undertook it, and the result was that in a few months he
completely broke down while out on a tour, and was
carried into Nellore, to all appearances more dead than
alive. No one believed it possible that he could recover;
but skillful treatment and careful nursing at the mission
house brought him up from the very gates of death. As
soon as he was able to travel he was ordered to quit
India. He sailed from Madras in September, and as it
would have been dangerous for him to face the winter of
England, he went to the south of France, where he remained till spring.

In the absence of a man to take up the Ramapatam
work, the field was temporarily divided between Nellore
and Ongole, while a circuit of ten miles was given to the

seminary. This arrangement continued till the establishment of a new station at Udayagiri which naturally took up a large portion of both the north and south sections of the old Ramapatam field. But this by no means sufficiently provided for what was the Ramapatam field. There ought to be, and probably will be at an early day, a station at Kavali, a growing and important town ten miles south of Ramapatam.

Ramapatam Theological Seminary has had a very important part in the work among the Telugus. It has frequently been said that if India is ever to be evangelized, it must be done to a very large extent by native agency. This is so universally believed that there is scarcely a mission of any importance in India that has not a "school of the prophets" to prepare natives for the ministry. Soon after Mr. Clough moved to Ongole, he began to agitate the question of a theological seminary for the Telugus. But it was not till 1870 that the subject took definite shape. At the mission conference of that year, held at Ramapatam, it was "Resolved, That a theological seminary is, in our opinion, an immediate necessity for the Telugu Mission." This, with several other resolutions bearing upon it, were unanimously passed and Mr. Clough was asked to correspond with the Executive Committee on the subject. The result of this action was that the Executive Committee sanctioned the request for the seminary and provided funds for the necessary buildings. By unanimous consent the seminary was located at Ramapatam, and this being the case the erection of the buildings was naturally entrusted to Mr. Timpany. The sem-

SEMINARY STUDENTS—RAMAPATAM.

inary was opened in April, 1872, under the management of Mr. Timpany, assisted by the native teachers. The number of students the first year was fifteen.

In the absence of anything like a high school in the mission, Mr. Timpany arranged the course of study to cover six years, the first three being preparatory and the last three purely theological. But this course was never strictly followed, and for two reasons. In the first place, the class of students sent to the seminary was not, as a rule, such as could take up the higher secular studies that had been prescribed. Some did take them up and pursued them with credit, but they were in the minority. The students were generally somewhat advanced in years, and some of them were married men with families. Hence, like students for the ministry at home in similar circumstances, a few years of biblical study were all they cared to take. Another reason was, the pressing need in the mission for preachers with even a very limited education made the missionaries impatient to get back the few that had been sent to the seminary. Still, the preparatory course was retained and followed more or less closely for several years.

In his first annual report of the seminary, Mr. Timpany said: "It is our purpose to raise up a class of fairly educated men, simple in their habits, with no artificial or imported wants—a ministry that the poor churches will not find it impossible to support."

The Rev. R. R. Williams, who had been designated to the seminary, arrived in Ramapatam, January 10, 1874, and immediately took the charge from Mr. Timpany. Although the latter remained on the list of teachers for a

short time, yet the whole burden of the seminary fell on
Mr. Williams. This was hard, for he was obliged to
begin teaching by the help of an interpreter. This at
best is very unsatisfactory, especially to the teacher, as it
gives no fair opportunity to get the language as a man in
such a position ought to get it. The tendency is that
while he may get a large vocabulary in a very short time,
he fails to get a correct idiomatic knowledge of the language or gets it only with an extraordinary amount of
labor. If the ordinary missionary needs at least the first
year free for study, much more should a man in such a
position. Moreover, there is a very decided conviction in
the mission that the man who presides over the theological
seminary should have a few years of active missionary
work on the field before taking up his seminary duties,
and thus learn by experience the real needs of the field
and the kind of training the students require. But we
have to do, not so much with what ought to be as with
what is. It should be said to Mr. Williams' credit, that
he entered upon his duties with great enthusiasm and succeeded better than the untoward circumstances warranted
any one to expect.

We have already referred to the successful effort of
Mr. Clough, when at home in 1872, to raise an endowment of fifty thousand dollars for the seminary. From
the income of this endowment the teachers and students
are supported. Unmarried students receive three rupees
a month, free quarters, and two suits of clothes each year.
Married students receive six rupees and clothes for both
themselves and wives. This is ample for all their needs,
and more than most of them are said to get after they be-

come preachers. The wives of the students are expected
to pursue the same studies with their husbands as far as
possible, and some of them have done remarkably well,
occasionally the wife being the better student of the two.

During the seven years of Mr. Williams' first term of
service he labored with untiring zeal to prepare the
students under his care for usefulness, and to build up the
seminary and make it a power for good in the mission.
He had many difficulties to overcome before success could
be attained. In 1876, he was sorely afflicted in the death
of his devoted and faithful wife. In this death the seminary also suffered, for Mrs. Williams was a teacher and
watched over the boys as a mother.

From very small beginnings, Mr. Williams was permitted to see the work grow and prosper far beyond what
even he had hoped for. As an indication of the aim of
the seminary, the character of the work done, and the
progress made, we quote as follows from Mr. Williams'
report for 1880:

"The seminary year is divided into two terms. The
first term commences the middle of July, and closes the
middle of December. The second term begins the first
of January, and continues until the last of April.

"The object of the seminary is to train its students for
the work of the ministry, i. e., to give the gospel to the
lost and build up believers in the great truths therein
revealed. Hence we give our strength to the study of
God's word. The *whole* Bible is studied thoroughly,
until its history and grand doctrines become familiar.
Much time is given to prophecy and its fulfillment. The
prophecies respecting the children of Israel, their cap-

K

tivity, restoration, the desolation of their country, and
destruction of their beautiful temple, and their dispersion
among the Gentiles, etc.   The prophecies concerning the
Messiah and his kingdom are traced from the first
promise made in the garden of Eden throughout the Old
Testament to their fulfillment in Jesus Christ and his
church, as revealed in the New Testament.   Special
attention is given to the study of the New Testament
during the three years.   The Gospels are memorized with
the historical portions of the New Testament, while the
Epistles are analyzed, and the great truths thoroughly
studied.   During the study of the pastoral Epistles, a
course of lectures is given on the constitution of the
church, its membership, officers, ordinances, and work.
We also deliver a course of lectures on church history,
beginning where the New Testament leaves off, and give
the more important facts of church history during the
earlier periods.   In order to give the students instruction
in sermonizing, we have two services a week for preaching.   The members of the senior class preach in turn.
The main object of these services is to give instruction to
those who hear, but we make suggestions and criticise the
sermons, to some extent.

   " At the close of each year, a committee of examiners
is present, and the classes are examined carefully in the
work of the year.   They are required to go over all the
ground, as far as possible, during the three days of examination.

   " The field within a radius of ten miles of Ramapatam
is cultivated by the teachers and students of the seminary.
There are thirty-five towns and villages in which there is

regular preaching as well as Sabbath-schools. We usually send out two men to a village, one from the senior or middle class with a junior. The former usually does the preaching and the latter conducts the Sunday-school. We have no building which will accommodate all of the students of the seminary and station schools, to say nothing of the Christians on the field. Three of the seminary teachers have been ordained to the work of the ministry. They are faithful and efficient men, bearing many of the burdens which heretofore rested wholly on the missionary. They visit the churches, baptize converts, administer the Lord's Supper, and instruct them in all things pertaining to the work of the church of Christ. During our few days of vacation we made a trip, going over as much of the field as we could. The interest was truly great. The students' work never appeared so satisfactory as now. They have done much hard work, and God has accepted it by giving them precious souls."

In February, 1881, Mr. Williams sailed for the United States. In his absence, the seminary was in charge of the Rev. W. B. Boggs, who carried on the work successfully till Dr. Williams' return in December, 1882, when Mr. Boggs removed to Cumbum, to open a new station there.

It was while Mr. Boggs was in charge of the seminary that the Rev. Dr. S. F. Smith visited the mission. For an account of this visit we again refer our readers to Dr. Smith's "Rambles in Mission Fields."

During Dr. Williams' sojourn in the United States, he secured fifteen thousand dollars for a new seminary building. This building is of stone and teak, and is a fine,

large, and substantial structure.   It has ample accommodation for class rooms on the lower floor, and over them a
spacious hall, for chapel purposes.   He also received from
Mr. William Bucknell, of Philadelphia, one thousand
dollars for the purchase of a seminary library, and from
other sources, money for the purchase of a press, which
has been set up, and on which a good deal of the mission
printing is done.

The continued illness of Mrs. Williams rendered it
necessary for them to return home in 1886.   They sailed
from Madras on the sixth of July, and reached home in
safety.   The seminary was left in charge of Dr. Clough,
who undertook to give it a general oversight, and to visit
it once a month to make the payments.   But the work
of the seminary was left with the native teachers.   This,
of course, was only a temporary arrangement till a new
president should be appointed.

The Rev. W. B. Boggs had given such perfect satisfaction during the two years he acted for Dr. Williams, that
there was a very general desire that he might be appointed
president of the seminary.   He had only been at home
ten months when the Executive Committee offered him
the appointment, and he immediately canceled the balance of his furlough and returned to India.   He arrived
in Ramapatam on the twenty-second of March, 1887, and
immediately took up his new duties.

The work has grown to such an extent that Dr. Boggs
felt he must have an assistant.   It was, therefore, a great
joy to him when his own son, Mr. W. E. Boggs, after completing his college and seminary course, offered himself
to our Board for educational work, and was accepted and

designated to the Telugu Mission. He and his wife arrived at Ramapatam December 15, 1890, where they
will remain for the present, and probably be associated
with Dr. Boggs in the seminary work.

Miss E. J. Cummings, M. D., arrived in Madras December 13, 1886, designated to Bapatla, where she
began her medical work. Her services were so much in
demand the first year, that she had no fair opportunity
of getting the language. She was therefore allowed one
year free from all work but study. This year was spent
partly in Coonoor, as her health had been far from good.
In December, 1889, she was again prepared for medical
work, but was now transferred to Ramapatam. Here she
had a good dispensary, and a growing practice among the
women of Ramapatam and surrounding villages. She
also had some Bible women under her charge, and made
occasional trips in the district on evangelistic, as well as
medical work.

In 1891, Miss Cummings was again compelled to retreat to the hills. For a time she seemed to have been
restored to health; but the improvement was of short
duration, and early in the present year, 1892, she returned to the United States.

CHAPTER XIII.

THE DECCAN.

THE term Dekhan or Deccan is from the Sanskrit word "Dakshina," south, and was originally applied to the whole peninsula of Hindustan south of the Vindhya Mountains. Later, however, it was restricted to that portion lying between the rivers Nurbudda and Krishna. Strictly speaking, therefore, Cocanada, Bimilipatam, etc., may all be said to be in the Deccan. But as the greater portion of it is included in the territory of the Nizam of

Hyderabad, the term is usually confined to his dominions. At all events that is the meaning given to it in these pages. Under this title will be considered our four stations, Secunderabad, Hanamakonda, Palmur, and Nalgonda.

The territory of the Nizam's Dominions covers an area of ninety-five thousand square miles, and contains a population of ten millions. Although the Nizam is a Mohammedan, most of his subjects are Hindus, and among the latter are over four millions of Telugus. The Nizam's capital is Hyderabad—from haider, a lion, and bad, a town. It is well named, if we may judge from the fierce, savage, and wicked appearance of its inhabitants.

Secunderabad is five miles distant from Hyderabad, and contains about fifty thousand inhabitants. It is a British cantonment, having one of the largest forces of British troops in India. Between these two cities is the British residency, a small city of itself. Besides the palace of the resident and a number of officers' houses, there is accommodation for a regiment of troops. The State is nominally independent, but practically is governed, to a large extent, by the British Resident. He is supposed simply to advise the Nizam and protect British interests, but his advice is seldom disregarded.

The Rev. W. W. Campbell, who accompanied Mr. Clough on his return to India in 1874, made a prospecting tour up into the Nizam's country at the close of that year, with a view to opening a mission station if it should appear inviting. He left Ongole on the 7th of December, traveling by road in a country cart, which enabled him to see much of the country and the people among whom he sought to labor. He reached Secunderabad on the

23d of the same month, and spent a week gathering what information he could. The impressions received were so favorable that he at once wrote to the Executive Committee requesting an appointment to Secunderabad. This came in March, 1875, and on the 23d of June Mr. and Mrs. Campbell set out for their new field. They reached Secunderabad on the 3d of July, and the following day, Sunday, they began their work by holding a service in the travelers' bungalow where they had halted. There were only four natives present. But this attendance was increased to thirteen the next time they met. Mrs. Campbell entered earnestly into the work, and succeeded in gathering from the native hamlets sixteen dirty and ragged little children whom she organized into a Sunday-school. Next Sunday she had twenty-three. She also opened a day school which grew until there were forty-seven pupils, when a panic was raised by a rumor that the children were to be forcibly baptized. This reduced the number to fourteen, but by Mrs. Campbell's persistent efforts the stampede was arrested, and by November the number had increased to seventy.

On the 14th of November, 1875, a church was organized. The constituent members consisted of a few native helpers from Ongole, and a few native Eurasian and European Christians of Secunderabad, altogether fourteen.

Although most of Mr. Campbell's time was occupied in getting settled in Secunderabad, he found time to do considerable touring among the villages. In these tours he was usually well received, though in many places it was the first time the people ever saw a missionary. Here and there he met with opposition, but he soon convinced

the people that he had come to live among them as a
friend, that they had nothing to fear from him, and that
he sought only their good.

After a year and a half of patient, earnest labor Mr.
Campbell was rewarded by seeing his first native converts
confessing Christ, in December, 1876. The first was a lad
who, after listening attentively and apparently taking in
the truth, rose up and said: "I will go and call father
and mother." They came, and all three were hopefully
converted and baptized. There was also an interesting
work among the soldiers of the cantonment, resulting in
the establishment of a regular English prayer meeting
and several conversions.

Toward the end of 1877, Mr. Campbell made a number
of tours among the villages. There was but one village
where there were any Christians, so that it was still pioneer
work, but with this difference, that wherever he had been
before the reception given him was much more cordial.
The single Christian family referred to was delighted to see
the missionary. After talking and praying with them, the
other villagers who had gathered round said that the first
time he came they had great fear. They fastened their
doors and remained concealed till he had gone. Now that
fear had all gone for they knew he was their friend. Sometimes the fear was that the missionary had come to get
money from them. They had no conception of a man working and traveling about the country at great expense who
did not get government pay, or who did not collect or extort
money from the people. Voluntary service and "all these
good words for nothing" was what they could not understand.

Mr. Campbell, like every other good missionary, laid much stress on colportage. He usually kept at least one man who devoted his whole time to selling tracts and Scrip· ture portions. He also expected his preachers to do more or less of this work, but as they labored chiefly among the lower class, few of whom could read, their sales were not large. The colporteur, on the other hand, went among the educated classes and sold many tracts and books. He also opened a book depot in the city, where religious and educational books were sold.

In 1878, a mission bungalow was secured in a very favorable location. It is near enough to the native population to be convenient for work, and yet sufficiently distant to avoid the nuisance of a too close proximity to a native village. In 1881, a building adjoining the bungalow was secured and remodeled into a chapel and schoolhouse. The holding of property in Secunderabad is peculiar. Being a British cantonment, all the land is held by government and can neither be bought nor sold. It is simply leased to the owners of houses with the distinct understanding that it must be given up whenever required for government purposes. In such cases, however, the government usually takes the buildings at a fair price, but if on account of the price offered, or any other reason, the owner refuses the terms, he is at liberty to remove his buildings, but must give up the land. In British India the land tenure is of two kinds. (1) That which is held by government and leased to occupants, and (2) that which is given or sold outright. In the latter case the land is as absolutely the owner's as property in the United States, and is never interfered with by government except when required for some such purpose as a railway, or other works that are for public good. In such cases the land can be taken up, but compensation is given not only for the market value of the land, but for buildings, trees, and every other legal or reasonable claim. Thus a strip of land has recently been cut off from the Nellore compound for the Nellore Railway. The land originally cost only two hundred and fifty rupees, but in settling the compensation, the question was not what it originally cost, but what it was worth when taken up, and hence it realized to the mission three thousand one hundred rupees.

For several years the health of Mrs. Campbell had been very poor. Every possible means were employed to regain health, and avoid relinquishing the work to which she was devotedly attached. In the judgment of some she remained much longer than her health warranted; but she was finally compelled, in May, 1881, to lay down her much-loved work and return home. She was carried on board the steamer at Bombay on a cot, and great fears were entertained that she would never see her native land. But she rallied on the voyage and reached home in safety, but has never been able to return to India. Mr. Campbell returned in November, 1882, and resumed his work. The Rev. Elbert Chute and wife arrived in Secunderabad at the same time, and began the study of Telugu, with a view to opening a new station in the Deccan.

In giving an account of his work for 1883, Mr. Campbell says: "I have been led, during the year, to realize more fully than ever the sincerity of the poor idolater. The example which has particularly impressed me is that of a carpenter, who has been considerably in my employ,

teaching the schoolboys his trade. He is a most devout
idolater. He has a room set apart to his household gods,
where he performs each morning his worship. I have
seen him at it many times, and he has shown me his idols,
and prides himself on his devotions. I have had many
talks with him. He acknowledges the truth, but does not
forsake his idolatry. He attended our chapel services a
number of times, and I gave him a New Testament. I
think I was leading him on, and that he was becoming
more and more interested, when his friends began to mis-
trust that he was being influenced, and opposition began.
He was taunted about reading the New Testament, etc.
He told me of this, and said : 'My relatives, of whom I
have many here, are all in this way.' As much as to
say : 'I cannot break from them and their religion.' The
power of caste and social relations is a mighty power of
Satan to keep souls in his grasp."

This is by no means a rare case. We know of one
identical in almost every particular, where a carpenter
expressed his purpose to be baptized, and even broke his
caste by eating with Christians, but at last yielded to the
seductions of Satan, and abandoned the worship of God
for that of dumb idols. Those who predict the speedy
downfall of Hinduism because of the wide-spread influence of education, Bible distribution, and even a mental
acquiescence in the truths of Christianity, little know the
terrible hold that caste has upon its victims. Mr. Chute,
in his first report, says : "Several of the caste people
have asked for baptism, but after learning that they must
sacrifice caste, have stopped to consider the subject."
And so thousands and tens of thousands of Hindus are

convinced of the truth of Christianity, but are bound hand and foot by caste. And yet, strange to say, there are so-called Christian missions in India that not only wink at caste, but even practice it. If there ever was a snare of the devil more bewitching and more cruel to its victims than another, that one is Hindu caste.

About six months of 1885 were spent in touring. During these tours many seemed on the verge of giving themselves to Christ ; but the great enemy was on guard, and in many ways so intimidated the poor people that they did not dare to forsake idol worship. Still the good seed was sown broadcast, with earnest prayer that in due time a harvest would be reaped.

In May of this year, Mr. and Mrs. Chute, who had been in the country two and a half years, and besides studying the language had done a good deal of direct mission work, removed to their own field at Palmur. Also in November, Mr. and Mrs. Newcomb, who came out to Se-cunderabad as assistant missionaries to Mr. Campbell in July, 1884, were transferred to Cumbum, to look after the work there during Mr. Boggs' absence in America. It was a great trial to Mr. Campbell's patience, as well as faith, to have these assistants removed just as they were beginning to be useful to him. But the work at Cumbum was urgent, and there was no other man available. Thus Mr. Campbell was left entirely alone at Secunderabad, Mrs. Campbell being still an invalid at home.

The most interesting feature of the work on this field in 1886, was the opening up of Nalgonda, which Mr. Campbell thought ought to become a new station at no distant day. Believing that this would be the case, he applied to government for a piece of land for a mission compound. This was secured, and a small mission house was erected as a sort of rest house for the missionary till a better could be supplied. The work in this section was most encouraging, and Mr. Campbell had great hopes respecting it. As we shall see later on, his expectations were not disappointed.

The Rev. R. Maplesden, formerly of Nursaraopetta, returned from his furlough and arrived at Secunderabad December 7th, 1887. Owing to the continued and serious illness of Mrs. Campbell, Mr. Campbell was called home, and arrived in New York June 7th, 1888. It is very difficult to understand why two such earnest and devoted missionaries should be kept at home, when the work they so dearly loved suffers for the lack of just such laborers. We must, however, trust the providences of God.

Mr. Campbell's departure left Mr. Maplesden in sole charge at Secunderabad. The Nalgonda portion of the field continued to interest the missionaries greatly, and in January, 1889, Mr. Maplesden reported the baptism of forty converts. This led him to renew with greater emphasis the appeal for a man for Nalgonda. The Board responded to this by appointing the Rev. A. Friesen, from Southern Russia, who, with his wife, arrived in Madras November 16th, and proceeded at once to Secunderabad.

The mission at Hanamakonda may occupy our attention for a little.

Hanamakonda derives its name from "Hanaman," the monkey god, and "konda," a hill; hence, "the hill of the monkey god." It is a town in the Nizam's Dominions situated between the rivers Godavery and Kistna, and is eighty-six miles northeast of Secunderabad. It is four and a half miles from Worungal, the capital of the ancient Telugu kings, and is built within the walls that surrounded that once famous city. The population is about eight thousand.

In December, 1878, Messrs. Campbell and Loughridge paid a visit to Hanamakonda, and were so favorably impressed that Mr. Loughridge applied to the Executive Committee for permission to open a station there. This was granted, and Mr. and Mrs. Loughridge arrived, and began mission work there January 11th, 1879. Although Mr. Day had visited and preached in Hanamakonda over forty years before, the field was practically new, so far as the gospel was concerned. Whatever effect Mr. Day's preaching had produced, had long since passed away.

After a year of labor among this people wholly given up to idolatry, Mr. Loughridge baptized his first convert, and soon after, four more. A church was organized on the 4th of January, 1880, and Sunday services and Sunday-school were established, and continued from that day on. A small day school had also been opened. Mrs. Loughridge entered earnestly into this school work and work among the women of Hanamakonda, and continued it for about a year, when her health completely broke down, and she was obliged to leave the country. She sailed for home in March, 1881. Mr. Loughridge went with her as far as England. Before he returned, Mr. Campbell had gone to England on the same errand. So Mr. Loughridge took charge of Secunderabad until Mr.

Campbell returned, and then resumed his own work at Hanamakonda.

The Rev. A. A. Newhall, after several years' absence, in the United States, returned to India in January, 1883, and joined Mr. Loughbridge in work at Hanamakonda. As the latter was busy erecting a bungalow, Mr. Newhall devoted his time chiefly to touring in the district. In 1884, after completing the bungalow and chapel, Mr. Loughbridge returned to America, leaving Mr. Newhall in charge of the work.

On the 22d of September, Mr. Newhall and Miss Marie Menke, of Madras, were married at Secunderabad, and on the 24th proceeded to Hanamakonda. In November, Miss Bertha Menke, arrived from Germany and united with her sister, Mrs. Newhall, in work among the girls and women of Hanamakonda. At the close of 1884 the membership had increased to sixteen, with twelve pupils in the day school.

Both Mr. Loughbridge and Mr. Newhall had made an earnest effort to make the work at Hanamakonda self-supporting. Hitherto the only two native preachers had supported themselves by cultivating a small piece of land, and preaching in their own neighborhood as they had opportunity. This may perhaps account, in part at least, for the slow progress that had been made. In 1885, a departure from this policy had been made in the appointing of two young men, who had received some training at the station school, as preachers on a small salary. The following year, however, one of these was thrown upon his own resources and the other partially adopted by the church. The next year Mr. Newhall reported that all the paid evangelistic work had been borne by the church. He said : "The quantity of such evangelistic work is, of course, much less in each case than if the preacher was supported out of mission funds; but the quality is, I believe, far superior to that formerly done under salary." He cites the case of one who had not even the name of being a "helper" and who, although he knew very little of the gospel himself, had been most zealous in making known that little to his fellow-men. On visiting the place five persons were found believing, and ready for baptism. They were baptized and gathered into a little independent church.

The opening of a railway between Secunderabad and Hanamakonda made considerable change in the station and the work. The bitter opposition of native officials gradually gave way, and the influx of European and Eurasian officials seemed to demand some efforts in English work. An English service was held on Sundays when the missionary was at the station.

The policy of self-support seems to have received a slight set-back in 1888. In his report, Mr. Newhall says : "The disadvantage of being obliged to labor without competent native assistants has been providentially removed, and we now have the services of two well-trained preachers, whose spirit and faithfulness have given us much gratification. They have been supported mostly out of mission funds, as the church members have been very backward in paying their subscriptions for the past year. Our third preacher, however, continued to support himself." Six converts were baptized during that year, making the number of members on the field, thirty-three.

Broken health compelled Mr. and Mrs. Newhall to leave their work and return home early in 1890. Mr. Maplesden undertook to look after the work at Hanama-konda, as well as his own, till a successor to Mr. Newhall could be sent out from home.

Palmur is a village in the Deccan, about fifty miles south of Secunderabad. The Rev. E. Chute and wife arrived in Secunderabad in November, 1882. After spending some time in the study of Telugu, Mr. Chute began making short tours in the southern portion of that field. The work opened up so well in the vicinity of Palmur that it was selected as a suitable place for a new station. He continued working the field from Secundera-bad till May, 1885, when he and his family removed to Palmur. Soon after arriving he applied to government for a piece of land, and secured some five acres in a healthful location.

A peculiarity of the work at Palmur is that from the very start the caste people appear to have been reached, and quite a number of the leading natives of the district were converted and baptized. A church was organized on the 28th of June, consisting of twenty-seven members. A school was also opened, which in a few months had eighty-two pupils. In this school a number of the castes were represented and it was open to all alike. This work, however, received a serious check the following year by the opening of a government school in the village, and a law was passed that all the caste pupils should attend this school. The mission school work was therefore confined chiefly to the boarding school.

But the evangelistic work went on with more and more success, even among the caste people. Still there was a great deal of opposition on account of caste, so much that the missionary had to resort to the courts for protection and redress. The authorities being friendly, the opposers were intimidated and the Christians greatly encouraged. Building operations prevented the missionary from touring as much as he would have desired; still some tours were made and everywhere with most encouraging success. There were now Christians living in about thirty villages of the district.

Miss Leoni Chute joined her brother in mission work at Palmur, December 5, 1887. This was a welcome addition to the missionary force and one from which much good was confidently expected.

Nalgonda is the fouth station in the Deccan, and the last that was added to the mission up to 1891. It is situated about sixty miles southeast of Secunderabad. The place was selected as a mission station by Mr. Campbell, who erected a small building as a place for the missionary to stay while touring in the vicinity. The Rev. A. Friesen was designated to this station, and after spending about a year at Secunderabad studying the language, he and Mrs. Friesen removed to Nalgonda in October, 1890. Mr. Friesen is supported by the Baptist churches of Russia. He is a man of excellent spirit, and from the first his work at Nalgonda has been prosperous. Forty-seven converts were baptized very soon after Mr. Friesen removed to his new station.

CHAPTER XIV.

KURNOOL, CUMBUM, AND MADRAS.

The mission at Kurnool. A deputation to Ongole. A tour by Mr. Clough.
Results therefrom. Organization of churches at Kurnool and Atmakur.
Postponement of baptisms. Failure of Mr. Drake's health. Need of
"spare" men at the missions. Reinforcements and mission promises.
Decrease of membership. Accounting for this. Mr. Morgan's account.
Want of mission chapel felt. Backwardness of education. Discontinuance
of mission schools. A significant fact. Possible causes of the mission's
decline. Mr. Morgan's illness and departure from the field. Assumption
of work by Mr. Silliman. A discouraging field. Changes at the mission.
Securing needful buildings. The mission at Cumbum. Mr. Boggs' appointment and re-appointment. Opening a mission station. The work of
training the converts. Famine impetus toward Christianity. Among the
Madagas principally. Idol houses giving place to schoolhouses. Lack of
a spirit of independence among the Hindus. Answer of caste people.
Native unconsciousness as to "ought." Need of a native reformer. Mr.
Boggs as a railway contractor. Enforced change of missionaries again. A
ripened field. Successful work of a new missionary. "Smaller fields or
more missionaries." A successful school A new bungalow. A large increase. Madras. The English foundation. Commercial importance.
Lack of harbor facilities. Reasons for the establishment of a mission
there. Beginning by Dr. Jewett. Zenana work. Additional forces. Need
of permanent quarters. Their securement by Dr Clough. A new compound. The construction of a new chapel. Costing a missionary's life.
Other changes. Caste schools Return thence of the Jewetts. Death
of Mr. Waterbury. The English mission church. Mr. Drake's pastorate.
Work among the women and girls General influence of the mission.
Mere numbers not its measure. Numbers in Madras likely to be small.

KURNOOL is on the Tungabudra River, about one
hundred and sixty-eight miles west of Ongole and
about the same distance south of Hyderabad. It has a
population of twenty thousand three hundred and twenty-
nine.

164

In 1871, several converts were made from a village near Cumbum, and subsequently others were converted from the same village. Early in 1875, a deputation came from Atmakur, near Kurnool, to Ongole, and asked for a preacher to be sent to their village. Two preachers, Paul and Guraviah, were sent and soon after converts were reported. In November of that year, Mr. Clough and the Rev. D. H. Drake, who joined the mission at Ramapatam in January, 1875, made a trip to Kurnool. They reached Atmakur November 29th, and next day Mr. Clough preached to a large number in the Madiga Palem. At noon a number of inquirers appeared at the tent, and as they really seemed to be converted, it was decided to remain another day. An inquiry meeting was held, and in the early morning of December 1st, twenty-six were baptized. The converts selected Guraviah as their pastor, and chose out from their own number certain ones to be their leaders or deacons.

On the way back Mr Drake was taken with fever, and continued ill for two months after his return to Ramapatam. In August, 1876, he removed to Kurnool. Soon after the great famine began, yet a number of tours was made resulting in the baptism of twenty-two converts.

The Kurnool Church was organized on the 23rd of December, 1877, composed of the twenty-two baptized in 1876, five dismissed by letter from Ongole, and one from Ramapatam. The Atmakur Church was organized on the following Sunday, December 30th, composed of twenty of the twenty-six baptized by Mr. Clough in December, 1875, to whom letters of dismission had been granted from the Ongole Church. Of the other six, four had died and two were excluded for drunkenness. The day following the organization thirty-one converts were baptized. A week later seventy more were baptized in another village. At the close of the year, three hundred were reported ready for baptism, but it was considered best to postpone the baptisms till after the famine.

In January, 1879, famine relief being all ended, Mr. Drake felt that he could no longer refuse baptism to those who for more than a year had professed faith in Christ and were begging to be baptized. He fully expected to baptize several hundreds, and had begun the work when he was prostrated with illness and was obliged to relinquish his field in the very midst of a precious harvest. He succeeded in baptizing twenty-nine at one place and thirty-five at another, and still others were importuning him to be received; but he had not the strength to continue, and reluctantly he had to leave Kurnool and proceed to Madras, from which port he sailed for America, March 25, 1879.

For a missionary in the prime of life to break down and be obliged to leave his chosen work is sad enough under any circumstances, but it is peculiarly so when this happens in the midst of a glorious ingathering. One is constrained to ask, will the time ever come when, in a mission like this, there will be a spare man to step into such a gap and gather in the sheaves instead of leaving them neglected on the field?

In December, 1879, the Rev. F. E. Morgan and wife arrived in Nellore, and soon after removed to Kurnool. There was as yet no mission bungalow, so that Mr. and Mrs. Morgan had to live in a small hired house, neither very comfortable nor in a very healthful location. This, however, was only temporary. An appropriation of five thousand rupees was made that year for the purchase of a site and erection of a mission house. This was completed and occupied in 1882.

During 1880, Mr. Morgan had baptized forty-seven, making the membership two hundred and ninety-seven. But in the following year the number had decreased to two hundred and eighty-three; in 1882, to one hundred and ninety-one; and in 1884, to one hundred and forty-four. It will be just for all parties concerned if we let Mr. Morgan speak for himself in accounting for this decrease in membership. Under date of July 1, 1882, he wrote: "I have for a long time known that there were many who showed little or no interest in the work of the church, and that unless they reformed they would in time have to be excluded. I felt that the time had come when it was necessary for the church to take action about them. The preacher at Atmakur, in whose judgment and piety I have confidence, and who is personally acquainted with the facts in regard to most of these persons, concurred with me. At a meeting in April, thirty-nine members of the Atmakur Church were excluded; and at a meeting of the Kurnool Church, the third of June, fifty-six persons were excluded. Previous to the June meeting, the two native preachers made a tour to the villages for the especial purpose of exhorting to Christian fidelity many who had long neglected their duties. Of these ninety-five persons, there are some who have not attended a meeting of the church since I came to Kurnool. Of those excluded, fourteen lived in a vil-

lage three miles from Atmakur; and though they go to
Atmakur frequently on market day (Sunday) they never
attend meetings, which are regularly held in the chapel.
Others were excluded for sins, such as drinking and contracting heathen marriages, in addition to neglect of their
church duties.

"In July, the church felt compelled to exclude a large
number who had for a long time neglected the ordinances. Very few persons, aside from the small number
of Christians resident in Kurnool, have attended the
Sabbath-school and preaching services regularly held in
the *mission bungalow*." We have emphasized the last two
words because, while we believe in the strictest possible
discipline, and that "neglect of the ordinances" is a sufficient cause for discipline, yet we think it possible that
neglect to provide a suitable *place* for the ordinances may
be at least an excuse if not a reason for such neglect. It
is now more than twelve years since the Kurnool Church
was organized, yet Kurnool is to-day without a chapel."

There is another peculiarity about the Kurnool field
which may, in part, account for this unprecedented decrease
in numbers. In the mission report of 1880, Mr. Morgan
wrote : "In the matter of education the field is in a very
backward state. A number of our Christians are fair
scholars, but are too young to teach. We now have a
good school at Kurnool, and are preparing a few young
men to teach, so that a want we feel so much will soon
be in a measure supplied." The following year the Kurnool school, Atmakur school, and two village schools,
were reported in a fair state of prosperity. But in 1882,
the report was : "The Christians, as a rule, show too little

interest in the maintenance of schools. The preacher at Atmakur, speaking of the Christians, said that their failure to appreciate the importance of sustaining a school gave him great sorrow; they had increased in sobriety, industry, and other graces, but in respect to schools they had not progressed. As I had taken considerable pains in having a teacher prepared for the school, I felt I ought not to contribute mission funds to support it." Hence the school was closed. Again in 1883, he said: "I regret that so little has been done in school work during the year. A few persons whom I would be glad to have under regular instruction cannot come, and others will not come at their own parents' expense." In 1884: "As to schools, very little has been done;" and finally in 1885: "I regret that there has been no day school during the year."

Now, whatever may be our theories respecting education in missions, it is a significant fact that the only station in the whole mission that has decreased in membership, is the one that has gone from "a good station school" and three village schools, to no school at all. It may be that a stricter discipline than is practiced in other stations is the real cause of the decline, but it may also be, in part at least, in an attempt to force a theory that is impracticable.

In 1885 and 1886, Mr. Morgan spent a great deal of time touring in the district, spending more time than he had hitherto done in each place visited. Here and there he saw hopeful signs that the gospel was winning its way to the dark and stony hearts of the people. Two converts were baptized in November of the latter year, and three

of the excluded members had been restored.   Only one
paid assistant had been employed during the year and the
Atmakur Church was without a pastor.   On the whole,
the work was still very discouraging.

Early in January, 1887, Mr. Morgan, who was then in
the Madras General Hospital for treatment for an abscess
in the throat, was advised to go home immediately.   He
with his family accordingly sailed from Madras, February
4th, under circumstances which gave rise to great fears
respecting his life, and very little encouragement to hope
that he would ever return to India.   He carried with him
the profoundest respect and deepest sympathy of the mission, and was followed by earnest prayer that God would
graciously spare his life and, if possible, return him to
India.

The Rev. E. E. Silliman, who joined the mission at
Madras in 1884, was appointed to take charge of Kurnool
after Mr. Morgan's departure.   As Mr. Silliman had
already command of the language, he was enabled to
enter at once into the work.   Two months after his
arrival, he reported having visited the larger portion of
the field, and having personally conversed with a majority
of the Christians.   He said that the country west of
Kurnool was a most discouraging field.   "The instability
of the first converts in that section," he said, "has
brought the church into great disrepute."   Other portions of the field, and notably Atmakur, he reported as
much more hopeful.   There were three churches in a
fairly prosperous condition, the least satisfactory being
the one in Kurnool town.

Mr. Silliman's health being in a very unsatisfactory

condition, and acting upon the advice of the best medical authority in Madras, he handed over the charge of the Kurnool field to Mr. Drake, and sailed for America on the 25th of March, 1888. As Mr. Drake had his own work to attend to in Madras, he could give but little attention to Kurnool, and hence this unfortunate field was left without proper missionary care until December, 1890, when the Rev. G. N. Thomssen arrived from America and took charge of it.

As Mr. Thomssen had some years' experience as a missionary at Vinukonda, he did not need to spend a year or two in getting ready for direct evangelistic work, but entered upon it at once. But he saw the need of some additional buildings, and particularly a chapel, before his work in Kurnool could be very effective. To the procuring of these he applied himself with every prospect of success.

Cumbum is a small town in the Kurnool District, and is situated on the Gundlacumma River, sixty-seven miles due west of Ongole. It contains about eight thousand inhabitants. Being near the foot of the Eastern Ghauts, a very bad type of fever usually prevails in the town. For this reason the mission compound is situated three miles out of town, in a fairly healthful locality.

The Rev. W. B. Boggs was first appointed a missionary by the Baptist Board of the Maritime Provinces of Canada, and sailed for Siam to join the seven missionaries who had gone out the year before in search of the Karens that were said to be found in that country. The search proved to be a fruitless one, and in 1875 the whole party was transferred to India to unite with the Upper Canadian Telugu Mission recently established at Cocanada. Six months after his arrival at Cocanada, Mr. Boggs broke down in health and had to return to Nova Scotia. In 1877, he had so far recovered as to be anxious to return to his work, but the Provincial Board hesitated to send him back. In 1878, however, he received an appointment from the Missionary Union, and in November sailed for Ongole, where he arrived January 27, 1879.

For two years Mr. Boggs was associated with Mr. Clough, and the following two years he had charge of the theological seminary at Ramapatam. On the return to India of Dr. Williams, in 1882, Mr. Boggs removed to Cumbum to open a new station at that place.

Cumbum is one of the regions which shared to a large extent in the great ingathering of 1878, so that Mr. Boggs did not enter a barren or unfruitful field. It had yielded large numbers of converts, and they were still coming by the hundreds. But while he did not have to spend long, weary years of seed-sowing before a harvest could be reaped, he had what was perhaps quite as difficult a task, namely, the training of the masses of poor, ignorant, and degraded Christians, who had come in with the multitude, knowing very little indeed about the principles of Christianity. This task was all the more difficult, because Cumbum was too remote from Ongole to receive much attention from the missionaries there. Many had relapsed into their former life after the first impulse had subsided. Others were in a luke-warm, indifferent state, while the majority, perhaps, were comparatively steadfast.

At the second quarterly meeting after Mr. Boggs reached Cumbum, eighty-nine were baptized, making two hundred and twenty since his arrival. Large numbers all over the field were reported as ready for baptism. The truth seems to be that here, as elsewhere, the great movement in 1878 gave an impetus toward Christianity, especially on the part of the particular class that was chiefly affected by it; that nothing can prevent the whole class in that region from embracing Christianity. Many of the people themselves say it is their fate, and they may as well come first as last. If the other castes were to any considerable extent affected, this explanation would not have so much weight, but so far the movement is confined almost exclusively to the Madagas.

Mr. Boggs spent a large portion of his time touring about the district, teaching and confirming the converts, and the result was a very much better condition of the Christians generally. The preachers needed a good deal of looking after, but, with proper supervision, they worked well. Remnants of heathenism clung to many of the Christians, who had to be rebuked, instructed, and, in a good many cases, excommunicated. On the other hand, many villages were visited, where even the heathen declared that they had no faith in the idols they worshiped. Mr. Boggs would then say, "that being so, you do not need this idol house—why not let us destroy it, and put a schoolhouse in its place?" and, in several instances, permission was given, and down went the idol house.

Referring to the caste people, Mr. Boggs said that everywhere they listened attentively to preaching, and confessed that Christianity was true, but he adds : "The

great want in the Hindu character is the want of
independence in thought and action—the want of indi-
viduality. The first answer with multitudes in all classes
and castes is: 'If the rest do so and so, I will;' 'If such
a leading man believes, I will; if he does not, I will not;'
'If my people should become Christians, I would.' Of
course it is easy, by a few illustrations, to show them the
absurdity of this; but while they laugh at themselves for
being so foolish, they continue in the same way. Very
few Hindus seem to appreciate the power of that little
word 'ought,'—I *ought* to do this, or I *ought not* to do
that. The times seem to be waiting for a Hindu Huss
or Luther. When will he arise and lead forward a
mighty movement? All the hopes that centred in Ke-
shub Chunder Sen have been blighted: he has finished
his earthly course; and he was not the reformer that India
most needs. If God should raise up an Indian Paul, what
multitudes of the caste people might bow to the truth!"

This quotation, besides giving a reason why the caste
people do not embrace Christianity, confirms what has
been said above, respecting the mass movement among
the Madagas.

The construction of a railway passing through Cumbum, presented an opportunity to Mr. Boggs to secure
employment to a large number of native Christians, and
at the same time of securing money for the erection of a
much needed chapel. He, therefore, took a contract to
build a section of the road near Cumbum. The chapel
was in due course erected, at a cost of about six thousand
rupees, every rupee of which came from the railway contract.

Mr. Boggs and his family were repeatedly attacked by the Cumbum fever, which few Europeans escape who stay for any length of time in that region, so that by the close of 1885 it became evident that they must relinquish their work for a time and return to America. In view of this change, Mr. and Mrs. Newcomb, who had come out as assistants to Mr. Campbell at Secunderabad, were appointed to occupy Cumbum until Mr. Boggs should return. They arrived in Cumbum in December, 1885, and Mr. Boggs and his family sailed for America in March, 1886.

Mr. Newcomb entered a field not only already " ripe for the harvest," but one where large harvests had already been gathered. To put a new man, with very little knowledge of either the language or the people, upon such an important field, was somewhat of a risk, but Mr. Newcomb appears to have managed wisely, and the work went on in a very satisfactory manner. His able corps of assistants, consisting of six ordained and twelve unordained preachers, continued their faithful labors, and two hundred were added by baptism in 1886. One of the serious obstacles Mr. Newcomb complained of was the large extent of territory the field covered, and the impossibility of one missionary giving it the supervision which effective work demanded. Smaller fields or more missionaries was what was needed to secure the best results. Three thousand Christians, and two hundred thousand heathen to look after, is certainly too much for any one man. And, yet, we have fields in the mission with double the number of heathen, and scarcely more than one-tenth the number of Christians, which ought to be still a harder field for one man to care for.

Mrs. Newcomb carried on vigorously and successfully the station school established by Mrs. Boggs. In 1889, this school earned a government grant-in-aid of six hundred rupees, and twenty-five of the boys entered the high school. This was very good work, indeed.

The year 1890 was by far the most fruitful and successful year of the mission's history, at least since the great ingathering of 1878. The number of baptisms was twelve hundred and six, which brought the membership up to five thousand and seventy. There were eight hundred children in forty-five schools. Mr. Newcomb spoke in high terms of the labors of his preachers, and of his able assistant, Mr. Peacock. An appropriation of eight thousand rupees was made in 1890 for the erection of a new mission bungalow, to replace the temporary one, which has served the purpose since the station was opened.

The city of Madras is the capital of the presidency of that name, and is the third city of India, in respect to size and political and commercial importance. It is distinguished as being the first territory in India owned by the British. It is situated on the Coromandel coast, on the western shore of the Bay of Bengal, in latitude 13° 5' north. In 1639, the English purchased a strip of land six miles long, and one mile inland, on which they erected a fort, and called it Fort Saint George, a name which, in official documents, the city bears to this day. For a commercial city, its location is most unfortunate. It is flat, and only a very few feet above the level of the sea, and hence its drainage is most imperfect; and yet, strange to say, it is not regarded as a specially unhealth-

ful city, as compared with either Calcutta or Bombay.
There is no natural harbor, so that until a few years
ago vessels were obliged to anchor in the open road-
stead, from one to three miles from the shore, exposed to
every wind but the west, and in case of storms, had to
put out to sea. Some eight or ten years ago the construction of an artificial harbor, or break-water, was commenced. When nearly completed, a large portion of it
was swept away by a cyclone, but the damage has been
repaired, and the harbor is now approaching completion.
Yet, in spite of these natural hindrances, Madras has
risen in population and wealth to the third place among
Indian cities.

Although Madras is a Tamil city, it contains between
eighty and a hundred thousand Telugus. Hence it was
that, in 1837, Mr. Day removed to Madras ; but he soon
after decided that a mission to the Telugus should be in
the Telugu country. After the mission had become established, however, there were many reasons why it should
have a station in Madras. Among these may be mentioned (1) the fact that it is the chief city of the presidency, including, of course, the Telugu country ; (2) that
it is the base of supplies, including the port of entry, for
the larger portion of the Telugu country ; and (3) the
fact already mentioned that there are nearly a hundred
thousand Telugus within its limits for whom there was no
mission laboring exclusively. There were Telugu schools,
but no Telugu mission. For these reasons, a station in
Madras has been earnestly advocated for at least ten or
twelve years past.

When Dr. Jewett returned to India, in 1878, it was the

M

wish of the Executive Committee that he should locate in Madras; but Dr. Jewett had a decided preference to return to his old field in Nellore. He accordingly went to Nellore, and remained there several months. In September, however, he was induced to reconsider his decision, and removed to Madras to open the new station. On the first Sabbath of October he held his first service in a small chapel in the compound of a house he had rented in Royapuram. The number present at this first service was thirty. Their plan was to conduct Sunday-school and service in the chapel in the morning, and to preach in the bazaars and surrounding pettas in the evening. Preaching was also continued in the afternoon of week days, and a prayer meeting held in the chapel every Friday evening. A day school was commenced in the mission compound, with ten pupils. Also one in Konde-tope, from which the first convert came. Zenana work was attended with some difficulty, because it was a new departure in that part of the city. Still, during the first year, six houses were regularly visited, and fourteen pupils taught. Both the school and zenana work was under the superintendence of Mrs. Jewett.

The Rev. S. W. Nichols and wife joined the mission December 5, 1878. Mrs. Nichols (daughter of Dr. and Mrs. Jewett), being a native of Nellore, had not quite forgotten all her Telugu, or, at all events, it came to her very rapidly; and hence she became a most valuable addition at a very early period of her missionary career.

The First Telugu Baptist Church was organized December 8, 1878, with fourteen members, who had brought letters from Nellore and Ongole. A number of additions

was made by baptism and letter, so that at the end of 1880
the membership was twenty-seven, and the pupils in school
numbered one hundred and three. Miss M. Menke joined
the mission December 13, 1880, and continued to labor
chiefly in school work till 1884, when she became the wife
of Rev. A. A. Newhall, and removed to Hanamakonda.

In June, 1881, the Rev. N. M. Waterbury was appointed a missionary to the Telugus and designated to
Madras, where he arrived November 7, 1881. Some time
previous to this the station had been removed from Royapuram to Vepery. But when in August, 1882, Mr. Waterbury took over the work from Dr. Jewett, the latter
returned to Royapuram. All these years, and until 1885,
the Madras work suffered for want of a fixed dwelling
place,—the missionaries having to live in hired houses,
and hence subject to frequent changes. By the efforts of
Dr. Clough, while at home, the money for two houses was
secured. The Madras work was thus divided into two
sections, according to the location of the houses.

From August, 1882, Mr. Waterbury continued the
work at Vepery, and also acted as mission treasurer during
Mr. Downie's absence in America. A second church was
organized October 6, 1884, with a membership of eighteen,
who were dismissed by letter from the Royapuram Church.
In 1885, Mr. Waterbury purchased a house and compound in Perambore, in the northwest corner of Madras.
It was thought by some that this selection was not a wise
one, being too far removed from the centre of the population, and the compound itself, though large and open, was
too low and wet and difficult to drain, and hence likely to
be unhealthful. But on the other hand, good compounds

in the most desirable locations were difficult to obtain and
very expensive; and in the opinion of the missionary,
Perambore was a growing section, and sufficiently near
the Telugus to be readily accessible. Dr. Clough made
a visit to the place, and approved of the selection; but
it was at a time when one of the chief objections to it
could not be detected,—namely, the marshy nature of the
land.

As soon as Mr. Waterbury got possession of the property, which was attended with a great deal of labor,
worry, and vexatious delay, he set apart a portion of the
house for a chapel and schoolhouse, so that the work was
not interrupted. He continued the out-stations that had
been established, and added to them. Preaching in the
surrounding pettas was continued daily, and the work
pushed in every possible direction. He had few assistants, and, with one exception, not very efficient, but he
made the most of what he had, and the work progressed.
But he felt handicapped for want of a suitable chapel for
the regular services, and hence began at once to lay his
plans for securing a chapel. The regular offerings of the
church were chiefly devoted to this object. As the amount
needed for the purchase and repair of the mission property
was less than the appropriation for it, he asked and obtained
permission to use the balance for the chapel. The building
was accordingly begun. We mean something more than
a figure of speech, when we say that into this work Mr.
Waterbury literally put his life. His means were limited, and he planned accordingly; but to secure the best
possible results for the money at his disposal, he labored
hard, and attended personally to almost every detail.

His zeal carried him beyond his p'ysical strength, and
it was while attending to this work, exposing himself to
the wet ground under foot and the sun over head, that
he contracted the sickness which ended his life. He
lived long enough to see the chapel so far completed as
to hold in it the last communion service he ever attended.
He had planned for the dedication of the chapel at the
annual mission conference, in January, but his own
funeral service, in November, was its dedication. The
chapel is a unique little building, in every way suitable for
the purpose. It is everything that could be desired, without a single rupee's worth of superfluous ornamentation
or expense.

The Rev. E. E. Silliman joined the mission in 1884.
He lived at Vepery till 1885, when he removed to the
new house at Royapuram. This house was purchased
for Dr. Jewett, and was selected by him as the most
desirable of the houses available in that section of the
city. It is in the midst of a native population of the
better class, and hence is well situated for work in that
particular section; but, like the Perambore house, it is too
far removed from the centre for ready access to other
portions of the city where Telugus live.

In 1886, Mr. Silliman's health became impaired, and
he was strongly advised to leave the Madras coast, and
find a drier climate. He was accordingly transferred to
Secunderabad, to co-operate with Mr. Campbell, but soon
after took charge of the Kurnool field.

During her residence at Royapuram, Mrs. Jewett became interested in zenana and caste girls' school work.
A caste girls' school was established, and a number of

zenanas was visited, and the women taught. In 1884, Miss M. M. Day removed to Madras, to engage with Mrs. Jewett in this work. At first, Miss Day took the caste school, but when Mrs. Jewett's health failed, Miss Day succeeded to the entire women's work in Royapuram. In this department she has had much encouragement and success.

Toward the close of 1885, Mrs. Jewett's health was so shaken, that her departure from India was deemed the only hope of saving her life. Dr. and Mrs. Jewett had been looking forward with fond expectation to a speedy return to the scenes of their former labors in the vicinity of Nellore. Since Mr. Bullard's departure from Alloor, no one had been permanently settled there and, on account of the pressure of other work, it could be but indifferently cared for by the missionary at Nellore. Appeals for a man for Alloor had so far been in vain; and as Dr. and Mrs. Jewett knew the field, and as Royapuram had been provided for by the arrival of Mr. Silliman, they applied for and obtained permission to remove to Alloor. But, in the meantime, and to the regret and disappointment of all concerned, Mrs. Jewett's health gave way, and they were obliged to return home. They left Madras in December and, after a brief sojourn in Malta, reached home in safety.

The saddest event, and severest blow to our work in Madras, was the death of Mr. Waterbury, which occurred on the 11th of November, 1886. Overwork, and especially the supervision of the erection of the new chapel, brought on an attack of enteritis, which after a week's illness ended his life. He was but thirty

years of age, and had just completed his fifth year of
missionary service, when he was called to his rest and
reward. The mission conference met that year at Perambore, when the new chapel was dedicated. The absence of Mr. Waterbury at this service made it exceed-
ingly sad and impressive. The Scriptures read on the
occasion were selections which Mr. Waterbury had chosen
for this service. The dedication sermon was preached by
the Rev. A. A. Newhall.

Mrs. Waterbury would gladly have labored on in
Madras, but her health was not at all good. She, therefore, left the following spring, with her two little children, and with great difficulty reached home in a very
feeble condition.

The Rev. W. R. Manley and wife, of Ongole, were on
the eve of returning home when this sad vacancy occurred in Madras. They were, however, induced to defer
their departure for a year, until some one could be sent
out to occupy the place. They accordingly removed to
Perambore in March, 1888.

The Rev. D. H. Drake, after an absence of nearly
seven years, rejoined the mission in December. He was
requested, for the time being, to remain in Madras, and
accordingly Mr. Manley handed over the work to him,
and, on the 9th of February, Mr. Manley and his family
sailed for the United States on furlough.

On the passage out, Mr. Drake became deeply interested in a young lady, Miss Alexander, who was on her
way to engage in missionary work in connection with
the Canadian mission at Cocanada. The result of this
was that Miss Alexander became Mrs. Drake on the

17th of January, 1889. The Canadian brethren were
greatly disappointed at the loss of so valuable a helper,
but what was loss to them was gain to us, and thus the
equation was maintained.

The Rev. Charles Hadley was appointed as the successor of Mr. Waterbury, and arrived in Madras on the
27th of November, 1890. In July, of that year, Mr.
Drake became pastor of the Madras English Baptist
Church, but continued in nominal charge of the Perambore work till October, 1891, when Mr. Hadley assumed
full charge.

The Madras Baptist Church formerly had some sort
of connection with the English Baptist Missionary Society. But for many years it has been, to a large extent, independent. Since 1882, it had been without a
pastor, but the services had been kept up by means of
pulpit supplies by missionaries and others. All efforts
to secure a suitable pastor had failed, and at length the
church was advised to seek admission to our mission. With
this in view, Mr. Drake assumed charge of the church,
and continued to labor in connection with it till January, 1892, when he returned to America. A few months
previous to his departure, Mr. Drake was sorely bereaved
by the death of his excellent and beloved wife. She
was a devoted missionary, and her death was a great
loss to the mission. The Rev. Mr. Beebee was sent to
Madras, to take up the work laid down by Mr. Drake,
until some permanent arrangement can be made. Besides
ministering to a worthy class of English speaking people in
Madras, it is expected that this enterprise will prove a very
valuable auxiliary in the general work of the mission.

The section of Madras where our other mission house is situated, has hitherto, in this sketch, been called Roya-puram. Strictly speaking, that is not correct. Roya-puram is where Dr. Jewett began the work, but the mission house is in Tondiarpetta, a little farther north than Royapuram. Here Miss Day, Miss Schuff, and Mrs. Pearce have carried on the work since Mr. Silli-man's removal to Kurnool. Their work is chiefly among the women and girls of that section of Madras. There is a boarding and day school in the compound, and there are schools in other parts of the city. A prominent feature of the work is zenana teaching and Bible woman's work. The premises are admirably situated in the midst of a dense native population of the better class. One or two preachers are also employed, so that, one way and another, these ladies are doing a very excellent work.

So far as evangelistic work is concerned, this much may be said at least, that after our advent a great deal more zeal for the Telugus of Madras was exhibited by other missions than had ever been known before. So that it would hardly be fair to measure our work by the few converts who have been made. If the accession of converts were the only or the chief aim of establishing a mission station, there are scores of places in the Telugu country where this could be much more easily secured. Growth in numbers will probably always be exceed-ingly slow in Madras.

CHAPTER XV.

ENLARGING THE BOUNDARIES.

New stations. Missions of other denominations. Denominational protests against territorial occupation. Baptist growth in the Kistna District. The mission at Bapatla. Advantages of location. Mr. Bullard's work. Formation of a church at Alloor. Mr. Bullard's settlement at Bapatla. Procurement of property. Importance of touring. Increase of school facilities. Baptisms from the Lutheran mission. Causes leading to this. Retirement of Mr. Bullard from the field, and arrival of Mr. Owen. Station at Nursaraopetta. Protest of the Lutherans. The number of converts demanding a station. A welcome more appropriate than a protest. Accession of Mr. Maplesden to our mission. Erection of buildings and organization of a church. Accessions and education. Perpetuation of the impulse of 1878. Subsequent ingatherings largely due to that. Breaking down of missionaries. Expanding work. Vinukonda. Meaning of term. Hindu tradition. Railway communications. Arrival of Mr. Thomssen. Erection of buildings. Tribute to Mr. Clou h. Need of Christian training. Native self-support. The true ideal. Distant yet as to realization. Numerous converts. Ripeness of the field. Missionaries not unopposed. A "heathen revival." Extract from Mr. Thomssen. Appeasing Ankamma. Heathen multitudes and Christian sowing. "God's army." Failure of health, and retirement of Mr. Thomssen. The work under Mr. Clough's supervision. Progress therein. Mission at Udayagiri. View from the hill near by. Significance of name, "Udaya." An answered prayer. Mr. Burditt assuming his work. Difficulty in erecting buildings. Isolation of the field. Hardness of it. Difference between a region partly Christian, and pure heathenism. Extract from Mr. Burditt. Material benefit influencing the people. Some fruits. Accessions from the Ongole field. Village schools. Brightening prospects. A sad bereavement. Appeals for a chapel. Securing one. Excellence of Mr. Burditt's work. Needed rest.

UNDER this head will be given a brief account of the new stations, Bapatla, Nursaraopetta, Vinukonda, and Udayagiri. The first three are in the Kistna District, which adjoins that of Nellore, on the north. Its

186

capital, or chief town, is Masulipatam, on the sea, and next to it in size is Guntur, near the centre of the district.

The first mission established in this part of the Telugu country, was that of the Church mission, in 1841, at Masulipatam. In 1842, the American Evangelical Lutherans established a mission at Guntur. We do not know whether it was the custom in those early days for a mission to claim the whole district in which it was located, nor whether the Church mission sent out "An Appeal and Protest" to all England and America against the encroachments of the Lutherans. If it did, we have never heard of it, just as our children will probably never hear of the one of recent date, which our Lutheran brethren issued when the American Baptists dared to follow the multitudes of baptized believers who demanded care in the portions of the Kistna District adjoining our own mission. But, however that may be, it is a fact that we have in the Kistna District more than double the number of communicants contained by the Lutheran and Church missions combined.

Bapatla is situated about twenty-five miles west of the mouth of the Kistna River, and forty miles northeast of Ongole. But the river delta forms a sort of promontory jutting out into the sea, and thus a bay is formed between this point and the coast farther south; so that Bapatla is within five miles of the sea, but with the peculiarity that from Bapatla it is to the south, instead of the east. This gives Bapatla an advantage of climate shared by no other station in the mission. The south wind, so trying in all other stations, becomes at Bapatla a pure ocean breeze. The population is about six thousand. In the Hindu temple there are a number of inscriptions dating back to A. D. 1154.

The Rev. E. Bullard, as already stated, arrived in Nellore in 1870, where he spent the first three years of his service. In 1873, he removed to Alloor, eighteen miles north of Nellore, and began a new station. This was one of the places selected by Messrs. Jewett and Clough for a station as early as 1866. A fine compound of eight acres, with a good garden and a house, which, with some repairs, might answer for a time, had been purchased. But Mr. Bullard thought it would be better to tear down the house and use the materials, as far as he could, and erect a chapel, which he could use as both chapel and bungalow, till a permanent dwelling house could be provided.

A church of sixty-six members was organized the first year, a majority of whom were dismissed by letters from the Nellore Church. At the close of 1876, the church had increased to ninety-seven, with an out-station at Atmakur, fifty miles west. This was very fair progress, but Mr. Bullard was not altogether satisfied, and he proposed to the missionary at Nellore to abandon Alloor, as a station, and make it an out-station of Nellore, while he should take over all the field work of both fields, outside a radius of twenty miles from Nellore. This plan was adopted, and Mr. Bullard entered the new work with a good deal of enthusiasm. But it was short-lived, for, in 1877, he returned to America on account of ill health.

Arriving at home, Mr. Bullard resigned his connection with the Missionary Union, and settled as pastor. In 1882, he was reappointed, and returned to India, and, for a time, was associated with Dr. Clough, in Ongole. When the Ongole field was subdivided, Bapatla was selected as one of the new stations, and Mr. and Mrs. Bullard chose it as their field of labor. Like the other portions of the Ongole field, Bapatla had shared to some extent in the great ingathering of 1878, and also in the impetus given to the work by that movement. Hence, during the first year, two hundred and fifty-three were baptized.

As there was no suitable house at Bapatla, Mr. and Mrs. Bullard lived most of the time at Guntur until the 24th of December, 1884, when they removed to Bapatla. After securing a site of some twelve acres of land, Mr. Bullard first erected a temporary building, which had to answer the double purpose of dwelling house and chapel for a time. But, eventually, a handsome bungalow was erected, at a cost of about twelve thousand rupees. A permanent chapel and other mission buildings were also constructed.

During 1886 and 1887, the number of additions was very much less than in previous years, but Mr. Bullard attributed this solely to the fact that his building operations had prevented him from touring in the villages. Two boarding schools, one for boys and one for girls, were established and carried on by Mrs. Bullard. Also two caste girls' schools, and thirty village schools were sustained. The pupils in these schools aggregated more than five hundred. To meet an increasing demand for village school-teachers, a normal school was organized in 1888. It began with fifteen pupils. Two hundred converts were baptized that year.

In 1889, Mr. Bullard baptized a considerable number of Christians, who had formerly belonged to the Lutheran mission at Guntur. From Mr. Bullard's report, we gather the following particulars of that movement : Some years ago a division took place in the Lutheran mission by the withdrawal of one of their missionaries, taking with him fourteen hundred members and fifty workers. For a time, this was practically a separate mission. But it was but short-lived, for the missionary soon felt compelled to leave the country and return to America. Even before he left, however, many of his people had asked to be baptized and received into our mission. The helpers and a majority of the people refused to return to the Lutheran mission. They professed to have changed their views on the subject of baptism, and, after satisfying himself of the sincerity of their profession, Mr. Bullard baptized twenty of the helpers and two hundred of the members, and many others were expected to follow. Of course, this caused a good deal of hard feeling among the Lutherans. But Mr. Bullard protested that it was from no unkind motives, nor any desire to proselytize or build up his own mission at the expense of another, that he consented to receive these people into our mission, but solely because he believed them sincere in professing a change of belief; and, under these circumstances, he could not do otherwise than receive them and be true to himself, or the cause he served.

In 1890, the number baptized was four hundred and

ninety-three, more than double that of any previous year, and still there were hundreds more said to be awaiting the ordinance.

The incessant labor and mental strain of the six years since the opening of the station, together with exposure to the sun, greatly debilitated Mr. Bullard's health, and, in the hope of prolonging their stay in the country a year or two longer, he and his family went to the Neilgiri Hills in March, where they remained till November, 1891. But he derived no permanent benefit from his stay on the hills, and hence, early in 1892, he and his family returned to America. Mr. and Mrs. Owen, who had recently arrived in Nellore, were sent to Bapatla to look after the work there.

Nursaraopetta, the second of the Kistna stations, is about twenty miles west of Guntur, and forty miles north of Ongole. It was against the occupation of this station that the Lutherans most loudly protested ; but, most unreasonably, as it seems to us. In the district around Nursaraopetta, we had some two thousand eight hundred and seven communicants, more than the Lutherans had in the whole district. To care for these converts as we ought, demanded that a missionary should be settled among them. In addition to this, there was the vast population to the west and north of Nursaraopetta which the Lutherans did not and could not care for. It was to supply this want that our mission entered the Kistna District, so that instead of a "protest," one would have supposed rather that a hearty welcome would be extended.

The Rev. R. Maplesden, who had been for some years pastor of the Madras English Baptist Church, joined our mission in January, 1882. Strangely enough, this resignation of the pastorate became the indirect cause of the church's becoming affiliated with our mission, for it was unable to secure a successor to Mr. Maplesden till Mr. Drake took charge of it, eight years later.

Mr. Maplesden remained at Ongole for some time, but went to Nursaraopetta, in 1883, to open the new station. He secured a piece of land for a compound, and erected a bungalow and small schoolhouse. A church was organized on the 7th of October, 1883, and on the same day one hundred and twenty-three were baptized into the new church.

This was a very encouraging beginning of the new enterprise, and Mr. Maplesden entered upon the work with a good deal of enthusiasm. He saw in his field what others had seen in theirs, the great need of training the masses of poor, ignorant Christians, and of providing primary education for their children. As to further ingatherings, he had no anxiety. He said: "The work has gained such an impetus that it will go on independently of the missionary." Perhaps some of the missionaries might not be willing to admit so much as that, but there can be no doubt that the impetus given to the work in 1878 had much to do with the subsequent ingatherings. In no other way can we account for the fact that these subsequent ingatherings have been almost exclusively confined to the same class of people, and to the same regions as that of 1878. In other fields, and among other classes, where equally good and faithful work has been done, there have been no such ingatherings.

Although Mr. Maplesden had been working in the Nursaraopetta field for a year or more, he did not remove his family until March, 1884. His stay at Nursaraopetta was brief, for, in April, 1885, on account of his health, he went to Bangalore, and never returned. After spending nearly a year at Bangalore, with little or no improvement, he sailed for England in January, 1886. Mr. Thomssen, of Vinukonda, looked after the Nursaraopetta work for about a year, when his health also failed, and he and his family returned to the United States.

The Rev. W. Powell, who was designated to Nursaraopetta, arrived in Madras, November 18, 1886. He remained for some months at Ongole, and then removed to Nursaraopetta, but he did not take full charge of the work from Dr. Clough till October, 1887. During the year, six hundred and sixteen were baptized. A boarding school for boys was established, which had fifty pupils. A caste school was also established in the town, but this was subsequently given up. On the field, there were some thirty village schools.

The year 1890 appears to have been a most successful year at Nursaraopetta. Nine hundred and three had professed faith in Christ and were baptized. Twelve separate churches were organized. A new chapel was commenced to accommodate seven hundred people, and to cost about ten thousand rupees. Toward this, the Missionary Union appropriated five thousand rupees.

Vinukonda means "hill of hearing," so named on account

N

count of the tradition which makes this the spot where
Rama heard the news of the abduction of his wife Seetamma.   The place abounds with Hindu remains of very
ancient date.   A railway has recently been constructed,
which runs through both Nursaraopetta and Vinukonda,
and puts these two stations in railway communication with
Madras and Bombay.   The population of Vinukonda is
about six thousand, and, like Nursaraopetta, it has been
one of the fruitful sections of the former Ongole field.

The Rev. George N. Thomssen arrived in Madras
March 4, 1882.   His first year was spent partly in Ongole, and partly in Ramapatam.   During this time, he
made two extensive tours with Dr. Clough.   On the 3d
of August he went to Vinukonda.   A good site for a
compound was secured, and a comfortable and substantial bungalow erected.   He also put up a neat little
building, which answered the double purpose of chapel
and schoolhouse.

Like the other missionaries of these new fields, Mr.
Thomssen spoke of the grand evangelistic work of Dr.
Clough, but saw the same pressing need of training the
Christians, many of whom seemed ignorant of even the
first principles of Christianity.   Building kept the missionary in the station much of the first year, yet one hundred and seventy-six were baptized.

At the July, '84, quarterly meeting, the missionary and
the preachers, after interesting discussions, arrived at the
conclusion (1) that the time had come, or was near at
hand, when the childhood of Telugu Christians must
pass away; and (2) that they must understand that the
work of the Missionary Union was to provide for the

evangelization of the heathen, while the Christians must support their own pastors, build their own schoolhouses, and take care of their own widows and orphans. The only mistake about this is the "time"; for after seven years, Vinukonda, and indeed the mission generally, seems about as far from that ideal as it was then.

In 1885, Mr. Thomssen made several extensive tours over his field. Everywhere he found the people ready both to hear and believe the truth. Four hundred and ten converts were baptized, and this was only a part of the hundreds who were asking to be baptized. The great body of these inquirers came, as in other sections, from among the Madigas. But there were some among the caste people a.., two of whom were baptized. The field truly seemed ready to be reaped.

But if any one supposes that missionaries are having it all their own way, and that the great enemy of souls is not fully awake to the danger that threatens his hold upon the Telugus, perhaps the following account of what Mr. Thomssen calls a "heathen revival," may tend to correct that impression. "While I am writing this, a din deafens me. Many tom-toms are being beaten, horns are being blown, goats and sheep are bleating, sky-rockets ascend, fire-crackers explode, people shout and sing. But what means this? During the last months many houses have been burned. The wily, wicked Brahmans tell the people this is the work of Ankamma. The wrath of this goddess has been incensed, and she is burning up the houses and the crops; and now the people are sacrificing thousands of goats and sheep, spending enormous sums of money to appease the goddess, and to feed the lazy, good-for-nothing Brahmans. The Ankamma temple is back of our mission compound, and so we are disturbed day and night by unearthly sounds. This feast has been in progress for nearly two months, and none can tell when it will come to a close. By this means, we have had an opportunity of preaching the gospel to thousands, who before this have never heard the name of Jesus. We have been sowing the seed; and we fully believe that in due time it will germinate and bear fruit.

"In my travels during the last months, in almost every village I have been met by bands of people, carrying an idol-house on bamboos, bearing torches, and every man, woman, and child having a staff with a bunch of leaves tied to the top. On inquiry, I have been told each band is *Rama dandu; i. e.*, God's army. So far as I can learn, this is a commemorative celebration of the exploits of Rama, in his war with the giant Ravanah. It is reported in Hindu mythology, that Ravanah abducted Seetamma, the wife of Rama. At Vinukonda, the mount of hearing, Rama heard of this; and seventy-two million monkeys assisted him in the war with Ravanah. This host of monkeys was called *Rama dandu*, or God's army. These bands of wandering devotees must sleep and eat in three different villages, on three successive nights. All castes, as well as out-castes, are represented in the ranks. The procession moves on, while tom-toms are beaten, and horns and other instruments are played. The people shout and sing, 'Rama, as in former days seventy-two million monkeys assisted thee, so we come up to thy help.' I am told that for forty years there has not been such a revival of idolatry as this."

Just as Mr. Thomssen was getting fairly into the work at Vinukonda, they were greatly afflicted in the loss of their oldest child, a boy of eight years, and of remarkable promise. This was followed by the death of their baby, and the serious illness of their only remaining child. These bereavements, together with the double burden of trying to care for the Nursaraopetta and Vinukonda fields, told severely on Mr. Thomssen's health. They went to Masulipatam in the hope that the sea air would restore him. But in this they were disappointed. Mr. Thomssen went to Madras, and was for a time in the general hospital, but acting upon the advice of the doctors, they decided to return home, and sailed for America in September, 1886. Thus two of the most promising fields on the mission were left destitute of missionary oversight. Dr. Clough took charge, but, with his own large field and the seminary on his hands, he could do little more than give a partial supervision to the native helpers of Nursaraopetta and Vinukonda. Mr. Clough's energy, as we have seen, was indefatigable, and his resources seemed to expand with every demand. But he, as others, has his limitations, and the charge of these two missions, in addition to his own, was simply too much. Again the need of "spare" men at our missions appears.

Since 1888, Mr. Kiernan, one of Dr. Clough's assistants, has been in charge of the Vinukonda field. From the reports Dr. Clough has given, the work seems to have gone on quite as well as could be expected, in the absence of a regular missionary. Indeed, if the number of baptisms is any criterion, the work never was so prosperous

Seven hundred and fourteen were baptized in 1889, and
five hundred and forty-three in 1890.

Udayagiri is a village of some three thousand inhabitants, situated about sixty miles west of Nellore, with
which it is connected by a good road.   It lies at the base
of an isolated hill, which rises to a height of three thous-
and and seventy-nine feet, from the top of which a magnificent view may be obtained.   On the east may be seen,
on a clear day, the silvery line of the ocean, seventy-five
miles distant; on the north and south a stretch of level
country, and on the west the Eastern Ghauts.   It is a
glorious place for seeing the sun both rise and set.   It is
this that probably gave the name to the place "Udaya,"
rising or morning, and "giri," a hill; hill of the rising, or
hill of the morning.   The hill was once strongly fortified,
being entirely surrounded by three tiers of battlements,
and having fifteen bastions for heavy guns, all in a very
fair state of preservation.   Down to 1840 it was held by
a petty prince, but on account of his suspected treasonable
plots the fortress was dismantled.

As early as 1851, Mr. Day, while on one of his tours,
selected this place as a suitable one for a mission station,
and prayed for a man to be sent there.   The answer to
that prayer was long delayed, for the man had to be born,
and converted, and educated, but at last he came in the
person of Rev. J. F. Burditt.

Mr. Burditt was originally designated to Ongole, but
was transferred to Nellore, to act for Mr. Downie during
the latter's two years' absence in America.   On being
relieved, in 1884, Mr. Burditt proceeded to take up his

new appointment at Udayagiri. His first work was the erection of a mission bungalow. This was attended with great difficulties and delays, owing to the absence of experienced workmen and suitable materials. Still, by persevering efforts, the bungalow was completed and occupied in 1886, and a creditable beginning was made in the work.

There is probably not another station in the mission so thoroughly cut off from civilized life, or a harder or more discouraging field than this at Udayagiri. It is literally in the jungle, and, although the missionaries of Nellore and Ramapatam from Mr. Day's time have made occasional visits to it, and now and then a convert or two, it is to all intents and purposes virgin soil, and very hard and stony at that. But there is nothing too hard for the Lord, and, as we shall see, even in such regions as Udayagiri, the gospel faithfully preached will find its way to the stony heart.

To begin a new station in such a field as this is a very different thing from opening one in a region containing hundreds and thousands of Christians. The Christians may be ignorant, and the task of developing them into something approximating a Christian church may be a difficult one, but still it is a much more trying and discouraging work to begin *de novo* in such a barren, heathen soil as Udayagiri. But there is, at least, this one compensation, that as Paul "strived to preach the gospel, not where Christ was named, lest I should build upon another man's foundation," the missionary in such a field as Udayagiri has that privilege, without striving for it.

In one of his early reports, Mr. Burditt said: "At

present we are surrounded by the thick darkness of heathenism. Pioneer work is not a thing of the past in this section of Telugu land, at least. The people seem to have hardly any sense of sin, or desire for salvation; no concern as to death, eternity, or anything future. Their whole thought in regard to our message is, 'Can you promise material benefit if I embrace this religion? If not, then we don't want it.' May we be supported by the prayers of God's people."

Mr. Burditt spent a large portion of 1886 in touring. He began this work on New Year's day, and on that trip preached in many villages where the gospel had never before been heard. His second tour was on that portion of the field formerly belonging to Nellore. On the 11th of July a church was organized, and ten converts were baptized. During the same year a section of what was once the Ramapatam field was handed over to Mr. Burditt by Dr. Clough. With it came a number of helpers, and quite a number of Christians. Mr. Burditt found that the Christians had suffered for want of proper watch-care, owing to their great distance from Ongole. Discipline was much needed, but this was wisely postponed to see what could be done by instruction and reproof.

The following year touring was continued, and the station work began to be more hopeful and fruitful. By the close of this year the membership had increased to three hundred. A small boarding school had been conducted by Mrs. Burditt, also a Bible class for women, and nine village schools were kept up.

The year 1889 opened brightly for the new station.

In every department of the work there was a very decided advance, and the missionaries were greatly encouraged. Forty-five had been baptized, but the discipline which was impending in 1886 seems to have taken place, as the total membership in 1889 was one hundred and seventeen. Besides a number of deaths among the native Christians this year, the missionaries were called to meet their first family sorrow in the death of a lovely little baby-girl. Alone in the jungle, they had to do for themselves and their little child those sad offices which are usually performed by others on such occasions.

All these years there was nothing worthy the name of a chapel at Udayagiri. Repeated appeals for aid in securing a chapel had been made to the Board, but for want of funds, or some other cause, no response came. But a chapel had to be built, or the work could not go on as it should. The Nellore Church contributed fifty rupees, and the missionary at Nellore provided fifty rupees more. Other missionaries also contributed, and the Christians of Udayagiri gave to the full extent of their ability. A friend in Canada gave several hundred dollars, and one way and another a handsome little chapel was completed and dedicated on the 12th of April, 1891. It cost only two thousand rupees, and considering its size, beauty, and quality is probably the cheapest building ever erected in the mission. In the material, as well as the spiritual sense of the term, Mr. Burditt has proven himself to be a " wise master builder."

After nine years of hard, faithful, and successful missionary work, Mr. and Mrs. Burditt had fairly earned a respite from their labors. But, even then, it was with

great reluctance that they availed themselves of the in-
vitation of the Board to return home for a season of rest.
Nor would they have done it, but for the fact that the
state of their health demanded it.   They left Udayagiri
on the 13th, and sailed from Bombay on the 18th of
April, 1891, for England, *en route* for America.

The Rev. W. R. Manley, having returned from his furlough, was appointed to Udayagiri until Mr. Burditt
should return.

CHAPTER XVI.

THE MISSION'S JUBILEE.

The Jubilee celebration. Held at Nellore. The selection of the date remarkable. Gathering of missionaries and others an inspiring sight. Address of J. Grose, Esq. Regret at Dr. Jewett's absence. An expression of
appreciation. Early struggles and present success. Permanence and stability. Recognition of the mission's efficiency. Recognition of progress.
An encouraging recital. Reminiscence of a visit to Ongole. Thanks to
Dr. Clough for educational advantages. School work and mission work.
Education of converts absolutely needed. Native evangelists should be
thoroughly equipped. A confusion of creeds in India. The native races.
The modified Turanianism, Brahmanism, and its system of caste. Mohammedanism and Buddhism. Progress of Christianity. Efforts of thinkers for a new faith. Present religious unrest and intellectual ferment.
Income tax and exchange. Necessary impartial attitude of the government. Opportunities for missionaries. An encouraging hope. Memorial sketches. Fitness of them. Mortality among missionaries. The
founder of the mission, Mr. Day. His field of labor. His discouragements and perseverance. His labors and death. Subsequent success
owing much to him. Career of Mrs. Day. Faithfulness in work. Surviving her husband. Mr. and Mrs. Van Husen. Excellence of character and
faithfulness in work. Mrs. Williams and Mrs. Newhall. Faithful labors
and brief careers. Rev. S. W. Nichols and others. Especial mention of
Rev. A. V. Timpany. His devotion and success. Falling in the harness.
Conclusion. Gratitude for the past. Vastly more to be accomplished.
Christ's travail and coronation.

ALTHOUGH the proceedings of the Jubilee celebration have been published in a small volume, en-
titled "The Lone Star Jubilee," this history would be
incomplete if it did not contain some account of that
most deeply interesting and memorable occasion. We
cannot, of course, reproduce the whole Jubilee volume,
and to discriminate and make a selection of a few

portions from so much that is excellent, is a somewhat delicate task. But we see no way other than to assume the responsibility.

The Jubilee was held at Nellore almost as a matter of course; for while the mission did not, strictly speaking, originate at Nellore, yet it was there that it first found its permanent location, and hence Nellore is the parent station. When the 5th of February, 1886, was fixed upon as the day for beginning the Jubilee, it was not known to the committee that had the matter in hand, that it had hit upon the exact date on which Mr. Day landed in India, fifty years before. Of course the members of the committee might have known, had they tried, but the fact that they did not know, and yet selected the exact date, seemed remarkable.

To see thirty-one missionaries from twenty different stations in the Telugu country gather at Nellore, the once "Lone Star," was a grand sight, which will not be soon forgotten by those who witnessed it.

After a devotional service (which preceded each session), the Rev. D. Downie, of Nellore, delivered an Address of Welcome. This was followed by Reminiscences of Rev. S. S. Day, by Miss M. M. Day, which are for the most part embodied in the early part of this history. The afternoon session of the first and succeeding days was given to services in Telugu of a deeply interesting nature.

Of the many valuable papers read and addresses delivered, during the six days of the Jubilee Conference, we have selected the following as perhaps the most important to the general reader, and which ought to find a place in this volume.

J. Grose, Esq., M. A., M. C. S., Collector of the Nellore District, addressed the meeting as follows:

"I must begin by giving expression to the general feeling of regret that Dr. Jewett is not here to take the chair this evening, as was intended when the programme was first drawn out. It was a great disappointment when the news came that he had to leave India finally, on account of the illness of Mrs. Jewett. No one could know the doctor without loving him, and what Mr. Downie and Miss Rauschenbusch have told us this evening shows us more than ever how highly we must value their earnest and devoted work, and the prophetic foresight and strength of character with which the doctor, foreseeing the ultimate success of the mission, resolved that it should still go on, when others lost courage and were inclined to take their hand from the plough. It was a graceful tribute to leave that flower-decked chair empty, in token that though our chairman is absent in body, he is with us in spirit. It seems to us especially hard that Dr. Jewett should have been taken away from India just before this Jubilee, which his work has made possible, and which would have given as much delight to him as to any one. The ways of Providence in this matter are past our understanding, but we know they are for his good, as well as ours; and our comfort must be, that though a good man and true has gone from our midst, there are good men and true still left; men who will work all the more zealously and devotedly because of the influence and example of Dr. Jewett.

"I must next thank you, gentlemen of the mission, for giving me this opportunity, on an occasion which belongs

absolutely to you, of expressing my sympathy with your
labors, and my appreciation of the results which those
labors have obtained in this and the surrounding districts. I need add nothing to Mr. Downie's story of how
God kept the mission together till the long and weary
struggles of the beginning passed into the success which
now attends it; but I must say something as to its permanence and stability, and as to the recognition which
the work of the Lone Star Mission has compelled. I
find its name well known in the remotest villages which
I visit. The aid which it gave to the people and to the
authorities at the time of the great famine has attracted
the attention of government to it, and established its
reputation as one of the instruments on which government
must rely in times of difficulty. The work it has done has
been so persistent and widespread that the consequences
can never disappear. The thousands who owe to it not
only a rise in social status, but a knowledge of the ines-
timable love of God in the redemption of the world by
our Lord Jesus Christ, the means of grace, and the hope
of glory, are not only a proof of its efficiency as an
evangelizing mission, but a security that its memory will
never be forgotten. All the mission wants is support,
and work so good as its work is, is sure to find support;
so that we may be confident that its existence will remain
unimpaired till its work is fully done.

"Our thanks are due to Mr. Downie for the history
which he has given us of the mission, showing how the
little church of eight members at Nellore, with its single
missionary, established as the result of nine years' hard
work after the mission had commenced, has developed

into the institution as we see it at present, with its thousands of converts, with its numerous missionaries, with its successful schools at Nellore and Ongole, and with its theological college, and what the sub-collector calls its cathedral—I have only seen it myself from the dim distance of the canal—at Ramapatam, and its chapel here. When I say *our* thanks, I mean the thanks of us outsiders especially. No doubt you missionaries knew beforehand the kind of story Mr. Downie would have to tell, but we, who are outside, knew less about it, and it was extremely encouraging to hear how strong faith, long-continued through stony paths, had led the mission upward and onward, so as to prove that the Lord of all power and might is with us still, ready as ever to help those who help themselves.

"The presence this evening of many of the faces I see before me reminds me of my visit to Ongole in 1884, and of the pleased astonishment with which I found active school work with hundreds of children going on in spacious buildings, public worship celebrated in a manner which seemed more fit for our largest towns than Ongole, and signs all around that a great evangelizing work was in rapid progress. I remember saying, when the foundation stone of this chapel was laid, that I looked forward with much interest and great hopes to the opening of the high school by this mission at Ongole, and I am glad to know that my hopes have been amply fulfilled. My thanks, as collector of this district, are due to Dr. Clough, who projected the school, who has watched over it from the beginning, and who has induced the generous people of America to give it a new building, now it has outgrown the first one. He has been ably seconded by Mr. Manley, but the credit of the conception belongs to him alone. I know of no place in this presidency, or, indeed, in all India, where a school of this kind was so much wanted, and it is a glory to the mission that it has supplied the want.

"I have already said that a great evangelizing work is in progress at Ongole, and it seems to me the proper complement of the scholastic efforts which are being made there, that the number of converts at Ongole is large in itself, and is increasing steadily. In this country, it seems to me that school work must be a part of mission work. I know that the subject is a well-worn one, and that I cannot hope to say anything new about it, but I feel it my duty to state my opinion, that the people who contend that all mission money should be spent in preaching the gospel, and little or none in teaching children, are wrong. The notion, it seems to me, is a notion which springs from ignorance or misapprehension of Indian conditions, and from undervaluing the power of caste. The converts who can be got at first are people whose children have to be taught good habits, and skill at handiwork, in order that they may do Christianity credit, and not disgrace it. More than that, the evangelizers of the future—and native members of the church must be employed as evangelizers before work so wide is done that the face of Indian society can be changed, and Christ reign triumphant from shore to shore—these native evangelizers must be furnished with all the weapons supplied by Western education, before they can compete with the champions of heathenism, and silence them. In most countries, the use of a wrong word, or a slip in grammar or logic, is as likely to result in the failure of an arguer, as a failure in truth; but this is more the case as regards religious arguments in India than anywhere else. India cannot be said to be a nation with a settled creed, or even a congeries of nations, with a congeries of settled creeds. Hinduism and Mohammedanism, with many variations of each, jostle each other everywhere. A thousand antagonists wait with ridicule, ready for each slip, when the gospel is preached. The champions of Christianity have to contend to a vast extent about the meaning of words and metaphysical conceptions, and nothing short of a thoroughly good education can enable them to gain the victory in such contests.

"As I have said, this is a country of innumerable conflicting creeds, jostling each other everywhere. To begin with, there are the aboriginal races with their idols, which are always of the lowest type, and often shapeless. Then come the Turanian and Scythic races, who are deep down in the social scale, but whose system is so leavened by Brahmanism that their religion can hardly be distinguished from Hinduism. Then come the Brahmans and the higher castes, who are at the head of the social fabric, and who have fashioned the institution of caste, and made it what it is now, the most persistent, conserving element of the policy which keeps them at the top, and the most watchful and inveterate antagonist of every system like Christianity, which attempts to do away with such distinction, and let the best man win his way up, whatever his beginning may have been. Among the other

O

religions comes Mohammedanism, which fights with all,
but has not succeeded in routing any. Among them *was*
Buddhism; but Buddhism, though it prevails throughout all the Eastern world except India, is dead, or almost
dead, in India, where it began. Last of all comes Christianity, which, if we believe our Bibles, we must be sure
will eventually extirpate all others. The state of society
is such that its progress must be slow; but, though slow,
it has been sure. Education is awaking the country, and
making its best men dissatisfied with Hinduism and caste.
Our government, in freeing the land from war and an-
archy, has given the people time and opportunity for
speculation. The thinkers are trying now, very naturally, to discover some new system better and higher than
Christianity, but we know they will fail in this; and
when they fail, and acknowledge their failure, the foundations of caste being loosened, and all eyes looking for
a new light, Christianity will come in and take possession.

"Yet in this country where, it must be remembered,
the conditions are such as to make social changes slower
and less frequent than they are in other countries, so
that they excite unusual attention when they come, there
is a vast amount of unrest and upheaval going on at
present. Noisy schemes of self-government fill the air
with clamor. The people of India, or rather of the
presidency towns, have tried for the first time to influence the course of a great election in England. Our
frontier has been shown to be vulnerable; though, thank
God, it has not been penetrated yet. A short and comparatively bloodless war has added a new State to our

great empire. The expense thus incurred has imposed
on us a renewal of the dreaded income tax, which is all
the more dreaded in these days when the rupee is suffering from the disease called 'exchange.' Curious religious systems are having their birth, welcomed with still
more curious enthusiasm. The education of boys has
progressed till it has created a public opinion, and the
education of girls has assumed so much importance that
it may be reckoned as a factor in the government of the
State. The government has continued triumphant so
long, that it may now safely assert its religion, though
it had so long to act as if it were of all religions, and
has still to preserve an impartial attitude. This time of
change is full of opportunities for missionaries, and for
none more than you, who, with the example of Mr. Day
and the other founders of the mission before you, may
be trusted to take full advantage of it.

"I must conclude by expressing my hope, indeed my
certainty, that this mission, which has now lasted fifty
years, will continue to the end the good work which it
has begun. I won't hope that it will have many more
Jubilees, for each Jubilee will mark the fact that fifty
years have passed away. But now, as I have told you,
affairs are beginning to progress more rapidly; vic-
tories will be more frequent and significant. The occasions for celebrating them will come more often, and
I trust that there may be many such occasions as interesting as this Jubilee, and even more full of rejoicing.
In the meantime, the missionaries will continue—and
they cannot do better or stronger work—to tell the
people of

" 'That God, who ever lives and loves
  One God, one law, one element,
  And one far-off divine event
  To which the whole creation moves.' "

This inspiring and appreciative address by the collector of the district was received enthusiastically by
those present, and others followed that were equally full
of thankfulness for the past and hope for the future.
The entire series of meetings, we may say, was helpful in
the extreme.

MEMORIAL SKETCH.

DECEASED MISSIONARIES OF THE AMERICAN BAPTIST AND CANADIAN BAPTIST TELUGU MISSIONS. 1836–1886.

BY THE REV. W. B. BOGGS, OF RAMAPATAM.

A COMMEMORATIVE celebration is held from time to time by the survivors of Balaklava and Inkerman, Cawnpore and Lucknow, to recall those thrilling scenes, and to keep alive memories of their comrades, the brave dead who laid down their lives in the weary siege, or on the blood-stained field.

Is it not meet also for the soldiers of Christ, who still survive, to recall the memory of their sainted comrades, to remember on such an occasion as this, their lives, and labors, and faithfulness, and love; yea, even their faces and their voices, not to canonize them, but to keep fresh in our hearts the Christian love which once bound us together in the service of our Heavenly Master. It seems right to place on permanent record the leading facts of their history, and the prominent features of their characters, albeit they are already on permanent record on "the tablets of enduring memory."

From the landing of Rev. S. S. Day in India, in the year 1836, to the present time, out of an aggregate of about *eighty* missionaries connected with the two missions here represented, *twelve* have fallen asleep in Jesus.

213

Of these, *six* died in active service in India, and *six* after their return to America.

REV. S. S. DAY.—This number includes the founder of the mission, Rev. S. S. Day. He was born in Ontario, Canada, in 1808 ; he received his education at Hamilton Literary and Theological Institution, was appointed a missionary to the Telugus in 1835, and arrived at Calcutta, *en route* to Vizagapatam, February 5, 1836, *fifty years ago to-day.* He was located temporarily at Vizagapatam, Chicacole, and Madras, and made earnest evangelistic efforts at each place ; but in 1840 he established the mission permanently at Nellore. In those early days progress was slow, for prejudice against Christianity was strong.

Those were the trying times of clearing the ground, breaking up the hard soil, and sowing the seed ; the times that test faith and patience. But through all discouragements and obstacles, he faithfully persevered in his work as a messenger of Christ to these idolatrous myriads. He visited America in 1846, and on his return to this country, in 1848, was accompanied by Mr. and Mrs. Jewett. On account of feeble health, he went again to America in 1853, and was never again able to resume his loved work in India. Then followed long years of waiting and suffering, his enforced absence from the mission field being very painful to him ; but in the beautiful words of Milton, on his own blindness:

"They also serve who only stand and wait."

He was, however, engaged as an agent of the Mission-

ary Union for two or three years in Canada, and, doubtless, the interest of Canadian Baptists in mission work
among the Telugus may be traced principally to his
efforts. He also served in the pastorate and in the occasional supply of several churches in New York State,
as far as his health permitted. After years of great
physical suffering, he at last peacefully entered into
rest on Sunday, September 17, 1871, at Homer, N. Y.

Will not many of the sheaves since gathered in with
rejoicing be reckoned to him, the faithful sower, who
went "forth weeping bearing precious seed?" Should
not the greatness of the superstructure enhance the praise
of those who, far back and deep down laid the foundation?

MRS. DAY.—Miss Roenna Clarke, who became the
wife of Rev. S. S. Day, was born at Stoddard, New
Hampshire, October 12, 1809. She was a true partner
of her husband's missionary labors and trials at Vizagapatam, Chicacole, Madras, and Nellore, and of his
subsequent ministerial work in America. Josiah Bur-
der, who became a faithful and successful minister of
Christ in the Canadian Mission, ascribed his conversion
to the efforts of Mrs. Day, when he was a pupil in her
school at Chicacole. In all the years that followed her
return to America, she always continued earnest in pro-
moting the cause to which her earlier years had been
given in India. She was also a prominent worker in the
Woman's Christian Temperance Union. She survived
her husband nine years, and died at Homer, N. Y., May
19, 1880. It was her privilege to be helpful in founding

a mission, which has since become known throughout the Christian world, encouraging her husband in days of despondency, comforting him in sorrow, watching over his health, and sharing with him in the patience of hope and the labor of love; and with him, the founder of the mission, she shares the high honor and the everlasting joy.

REV. STEPHEN VAN HUSEN.—Mr. Van Husen was born at Catskill, N. Y., December 5, 1812; was educated at Hamilton Literary and Theological Institution; sailed for India in 1839, and arrived at Nellore March 21, 1840. His missionary service extended to five years only, failing health leading him to return to America in 1845. The data necessary for a more detailed sketch of his life are not available. He was associated with Mr. Day here at Nellore, and was a faithful, devoted man. His death took place December 13, 1854, at Brattleboro, Vermont.

MRS. VAN HUSEN.—Of Mrs. Van Husen's history, we have been able to gather a few facts only. She was born at Lima, N. Y., March 10, 1811. We have it on the testimony of one who knows, that she was a most excellent woman and devoted missionary, and that she regarded her leaving the mission work as the greatest trial of her life. She died, we believe, at Niagara Falls, N. Y., but the date is uncertain.

MRS. WILLIAMS.—The next name on the roll of these sainted ones brings us down to quite a recent date in the history. It is that of Mrs. V. R. Williams, a name of precious memory. For the facts, we are indebted chiefly to the beautiful tribute prepared by Mrs. Clough at the time of Mrs. Williams' death :

MISS VINA RUTH CLOUGH was born in Winnebago County, Illinois, in the year 1845, but in her childhood removed with her parents to the State of Iowa, where her youth was spent. Being brought to the knowledge of Christ's love, she became a living, active Christian, and at the time of her brother's dedication to the missionary service in 1864, she felt the stirrings of the missionary spirit in her heart; and from that time was desirous to be engaged in efforts for the salvation of souls. She earnestly sought for mental improvement, and attained her purpose in a very encouraging degree.

In 1873, she was married to Rev. R. R. Williams, then under appointment to the Telugu Mission as principal of the theological seminary at Ramapatam. They arrived in this country in December, 1873. Being very energetic and earnest, she entered with her whole heart into the work which lay before her. She was not content to be simply the wife of a missionary, but was a missionary herself, the strong current of her sympathies going out toward all around her, and her zeal manifesting itself in devoted labors. She assisted much in the instruction of the students.

But in three years her brief course was ended. On the 3rd of June, 1876, she died in Madras, her sudden removal filling many hearts with sorrow, and leaving a mournful blank at Ramapatam. Her body was brought back to Ramapatam, and laid to rest near the scene of her devoted efforts.

Mrs. Newhall.—The next year, 1877, took another from our ranks in the prime of life, and usefulness, and hope,—Mrs. Newhall, of Ramapatam. Miss Mary A. Wood was born at Bridgewater, England, in July, 1845. She went as a child to America with her parents, and lived at Belvidere, Illinois. It was there that she professed faith in Christ. In 1867, she graduated at the Rockford Female Seminary. At that time, she was longing to be engaged in mission work, and was considering the question of coming to India, but her health did not then seem to warrant it. But after spending several years in teaching, she offered herself for foreign mission service, and was accepted by the Woman's Society of the West. She sailed from New York, September 19, 1874, and reached Nellore January 2, 1875. In March, of the same year, she went to Ramapatam, and was there associated with Miss Peabody in the work of female education.

On the 19th of July, 1876, she was married to Rev. A. A. Newhall, and with him shared in the mission work, and in the special toils and trials which the terrible famine of 1877 brought. She was seriously ill on several occasions, each of which left her in a more precarious state. At length, she was brought to Nellore for medical treatment, and for a time encouraging hopes were entertained regarding her. But a change came, and although all was done that love and skill could do, on the 9th of October, 1877, she passed away to the better land. Her remains were interred in the Nellore Cemetery. Judged by the standard of months and years, her service was short; but reckoned by her heart's love for perishing souls, and her sincere consecration to the work of bringing them to Christ, it was long.

REV. S. W. NICHOLS.—He was born in Vermont, and at his conversion became a member of the church in Burlington. He studied at Madison University, and was ordained at Brookfield, N. Y., September 26, 1877. After spending a year in the pastorate, he offered himself for foreign missionary service, and in pursuance of his appointment, reached India in company with Mrs. Nichols in December, 1878. He was stationed at Madras, to labor in co-operation with his father-in-law, Dr. Jewett. He entered on the work of preparation with earnest purpose, but most of the time he was struggling to bear up under increasing disease. The last few months of his life were spent amid much depression and suffering. On December 8, 1880, having been only two years in India, he died at Madras, aged about thirty-four years.

MRS. NICHOLS.—Miss Hattie Jewett, wife of Rev. S. W. Nichols, and daughter of Dr. and Mrs. Jewett, was born at Nellore, in 1854. She went to America with her parents when she was nearly seven years old, where she remained until her return to this country as Mrs. Nichols. She graduated from the high school at Grand Rapids, Michigan, and the normal school at Oswego, N. Y.

Having spent her earlier years in this country, the
Telugu language came to her more readily on her return,
and she was able to enter upon zenana teaching and
other branches of mission work comparatively soon.
Her energy and ability gave promise of much usefulness, but in 1831 her health began to decline, and she
gradually sank until, on the 17th day of December,
1881, a year after the death of her husband, she passed
beyond the veil, at the age of twenty-seven. Her rest-
ing-place is by that of her husband, in the Pursewaukum
Cemetery, at Madras.

REV. D. K. RAYL.—A feeling of peculiar sadness is
awakened by the recollection of this dear brother; his
earnest purposes and plans ended in such early disappointment. With him, the sun went down while it was
high noon. He was in India only about one year and
a half, and the latter part of that period was spent in
struggling with an incurable malady.

Brother Rayl was born at Fredericksburg, Ohio, January 8, 1849. Soon after his conversion, he felt drawn
toward the work of the Christian ministry. Desiring
mental culture, he succeeded in taking a course of study
at Denison University, Granville, Ohio, and subsequently
at the theological seminary at Morgan Park. Respond-
ing to the earnest call for more laborers in the Telugu
missions, he received an appointment, was ordained August 16, 1882, and with Mrs. Rayl, landed in India in
November, 1882. He was located at Ongole, and besides
studying the Telugu language, assisted in the work of
the mission as he was able, especially after Dr. Clough's

departure for America in October, 1883. He was also active in the maintenance of English religious services.

He was a truly pious and faithful man, but physically unfit for this service. Early in 1884, the disease (consumption), which had long been undermining his strength, became violent, and quite prostrated him. Being compelled to give up all hope of usefulness, and even life in India, he, with his wife and their little child, set out for America, hoping, if possible, to reach the dear old home before the end should come. And he did live to reach home, though in extreme prostration. But a few days afterward he fell asleep in Jesus. His death took place at Millbrook, Ohio, September 10, 1884, twenty-four days after they landed at New York.

Mrs. Rayl.—Her maiden name was Miss Lily Johnson. Most of the items of her missionary career have been already given in the sketch of Mr. Rayl's life. But we may add that she was born in Illinois, April 1, 1859. Early in life she wished to fit herself for usefulness, and so followed a course of study at Granville Ladies' Seminary. Afterward she spent some time as a mission teacher among the freedmen in the city of Richmond, Va. She was a bright, spirited, active person, and delighted in the service of Christ. As the wife of Brother Rayl she came to India, a true helpmeet, sharing his purposes, his efforts, his trials, and disappointments. She also went as an invalid when they returned to America, and survived her husband only twenty days. She died at her mother's home at Sunbury, Ohio, September 30, 1884, leaving a babe only a few months old.

It was in their hearts to serve God in India, but such service was not long permitted them.   And it is the heart that God takes special cognizance of.

REV. A. V. TIMPANY.—Most prominent and useful among the workers in India was Rev. A. V. Timpany. He was a burning and a shining light in both these missions, and his name will long remain sacredly enshrined in the memories of his co-laborers both in India and America, and also in the hearts of multitudes of Telugu Christians.

He was born at Vienna, Ontario, Canada, December 21, 1840; was educated at the Woodstock Institute, ordained at Brantford, October 14, 1867, and being called of God to the foreign missionary service, came to India under appointment of the American Baptist Missionary Union. He and his wife landed at Madras in April, 1868. After spending the period of preparation at Nellore, he removed in February, 1870, to Ramapatam, where he opened a new station, and cultivated the field with great devotion and marked success. The name of A. V. Timpany seems inseparably connected with Ramapatam. When the theological seminary was commenced in April, 1872, Brother Timpany was put in charge of it as temporary principal until Rev. R. R. Williams was sent out especially for that work. Being an assiduous student of the Telugu language, and deeply interested in Bible work and all measures designed to uplift and bless the people, he was chosen as one of the Telugu Revision Committee of the Madras Auxiliary Bible Society. He devoted to literary efforts the time that could be spared from his active evangelistic work, and prepared and published a "Compendium of Theology" in Telugu.

In 1876, he and his family went to America on furlough, and while at home his transfer from the American to the Canadian Mission was effected most amicably. After rendering very efficient service to the mission during his stay in Canada, he returned under the auspices of the Board of Ontario and Quebec. He arrived in India, the second time, in December, 1878, and was stationed at Cocanada, Mr. McLaurin removing to Samulcotta to take charge of the newly established seminary. Re-entering upon the mission work with his accustomed zeal and vigor, he continued to sow the seed and reap the harvest, to pray, and rejoice, and hope, until called to rest. To him the call came very suddenly. On the 19th of February, 1885, at his home at Cocanada, in a few hours he passed from his usual state of health to the grave. In the morning he was seized with cholera, and in the evening was buried.

A noble-spirited man ; a zealous, faithful, wise, successful missionary ; a warm-hearted, true friend! The tidings of his sudden departure sent a peculiarly sharp pang of grief through all our hearts throughout all the borders of the Telugu Mission. But to whom, if not to him, shall the Master's approval be spoken, "Well done, good and faithful servant!"

MRS. DRAKE.—Mrs. Drake was born June 20, 1854, near Niagara, Canada. She was a daughter of Rev. John Alexander, at present pastor of one of the Baptist churches in Toronto. She came to India as Miss Isabella

Alexander. She had the full confidence of the Baptist
Missionary Society of Ontario and Quebec, under whose
auspices she was sent out, was beloved by members in the
churches wherever she was known, and was followed by
their prayers. She sailed from Boston October 6, 1887.
On the 17th of January, 1888, she was married at Cocanada, to Rev. D. H. Drake, of the American Baptist
Telugu Mission, and soon after settled at Perambore,
Madras, where Mr. Drake was stationed. Here she entered at once on the study of the Telugu language, and
engaged in active Christian work wherever an opportunity
offered, and here, for three years, she gave herself most
earnestly and faithfully to the work of Telugu evangelization and instruction. When Mr. Drake took the pastorate of the English-speaking Baptist church in Vepery,
Madras, they removed to that part of the city, and there
she continued to labor assiduously up to the last, both
as a pastor's wife and as a missionary. On Sunday, September 20th, she taught her Sunday-school class as usual
in the afternoon, came home feeling ill, was seized with
cholera, and on Monday morning met death with perfect
resignation and Christian hope. Her body rests in St.
Andrew's Cemetery, Madras, near the grave of another
devoted Telugu missionary, Rev. N. M. Waterbury, who
fell asleep in Jesus at Perambore, in November, 1886.

As a friend, Mrs. Drake was genial, hospitable, warm-
hearted; as a missionary, earnest, faithful, and loving,
constantly engaged in the work for which the Lord
called her to India. Beloved by all her fellow missionaries, both in her own society and in others, and by
all the native Christians who came within the range of

her sympathetic and earnest efforts, she is sincerely mourned throughout the length and breadth of the Telugu Mission. She has passed on to the rest that remaineth for the people of God.

Thus these loved ones lived and died, but they are *in Him*, who is " alive for evermore." To us there is sadness, but to them the eternal song We are still in the land of the dying, while they have reached the land of the living. To us there is still the cross, to them the fadeless crown. All glory to God, in whom they believed, and through whom their lives were beautiful and useful, who called them to his service and to eternal salvation !

With us their names shall live
Through long succeeding years,
Embalmed with all our hearts can give,
Our praises and our tears.

It is not death to die,—
To leave this weary road,
And 'mid the brotherhood on high,
To be at home with God.

It is not death to close
The eye long dimmed by tears,
And wake in glorious repose,
To spend eternal years.

It is not death to fling
Aside this sinful dust,
And rise on strong, exulting wing,
To live among the just.

Jesus, thou Prince of life,
Thy chosen cannot die,
Like thee, they conquer in the strife,
To reign with thee on high.

P

We have reached the end of our allotted task.   The
results of these fifty-six years of seed-sowing and harvest
among the Telugus are ample to call forth our profoundest gratitude to the God of missions.   But it should also
be borne in mind that what has been done, is as nothing
compared to what yet remains to be accomplished.   Not
yet can the Saviour " see of the travail of his soul and be
satisfied."   Nor will he, until these thousands who have
been redeemed shall be multiplied by tens and hundreds
of thousands—nay, not till this whole Telugu people
shall be brought to Christ, and he by them be " crowned
Lord of all."

THE END.

GENERAL INDEX.

227

www.ingramcontent.com/pod-product-compliance
Lightning Source LLC
Chambersburg PA
CBHW030355270326
41926CB00009B/1119